Africa for Kids

Exploring a Vibrant Continent

☀ 19 Activities ☀

Harvey Croze

CHICAGO
REVIEW
PRESS

Cover and interior design: Rattray Design
Interior illustrations: Laura D'Argo

Image credits
Front and back cover images courtesy of Photodisc, except photo
    of African children, courtesy of Corbis, and elephants, by
    Harvey Croze.

pages i, 36, and 37 (hippos) courtesy of Photodisc
pages vi (smiling group), 40 (leopard), 70, 73, 104, 108, 109, 110,
    114 (schoolchildren), 122, and 125 © CameraPix Ltd.
pages 3, 11, 13, and 23 adapted from maps by Africa Interactive
    Maps
page 12: data provided by USGS, compiled by UNEP/GRID—Sioux
    Falls
pages 25, 28, 40 (buffalo), 41, 53 (lioness), 54 (ant, weevil, slug),
    55 (weaverbird), and 56 (Burchell's zebra) courtesy of John
    Reader
pages 31 and 34 courtesy of Digital Vision
page 32 courtesy of Justo Casal
pages 33, 83, 93 (Dogon dancers), 102, and 114 (Swazi king)
    © Carol Beckwith/Angela Fisher: Robert Estall Agency
page 46: pyramid of life illustration by Maya Geheb
page 47: two-headed nkondi courtesy of Imprimerie Nationale,
    Paris; buffalo mask courtesy of Schirner Verlag, Darmstadt
page 50: hyena mask and snake statue courtesy of Museum for
    African Art, New York; junk owl by Kioko
pages 55 (elephants playing) and 94 courtesy of Cynthia Moss
page 57 courtesy of Taxi/Ken Ross
page 60 courtesy of The Image Bank/David Sacks
pages 63, 64, and 71 courtesy of David Coulson, Trust for African
    Rock Art
page 79 adapted from a drawing by Carol Beckwith
page 93 courtesy of Stockbyte
page 106: original painting by Osman
page 111 adapted from a map © United Nations Development
    Programmme
page 119 courtesy of Hulton Archive/Kenneth Rittener
page 127 courtesy of Reportage/Tom Stoddart

All other images by the author or from the author's collection.

Library of Congress Cataloging-in-Publication Data
Croze, Harvey.
    Africa for kids : exploring a vibrant continent, 19 activities / Harvey
Croze.— 1st ed.
        p. cm.
    Includes bibliographical references and index.
    ISBN-13: 978-1-55652-598-8
    ISBN-10: 1-55652-598-2
    1. Africa—Juvenile literature. 2. Africa—Study and teaching—Activity
programs. I. Title.
DT22.C76 2006
916—dc22
                                                            2005031828

© 2006 by Harvey Croze
First edition
Published by Chicago Review Press, Incorporated
814 North Franklin Street
Chicago, Illinois 60610
ISBN-13: 978-1-55652-598-8
ISBN-10: 1-55652-598-2
Printed in China
5 4 3

For Katya, Taro, Kaia, Leon, Talu, Myla, and
all the other kids who share an African future

"Children are the most vulnerable members of any society and our greatest treasures. In South Africa children must be able to play once again. They must no longer suffer hunger and disease, threatened by the scourge of ignorance, molestation, and abuse. And they should no longer be forced to engage in deeds whose gravity exceeds their tender years. They suffered too long when they sacrificed everything for liberty, peace, human dignity, and human fulfillment."

—Nelson Mandela, former president
of the Republic of South Africa

Contents

Introduction
What Is Africa?

Africa is huge. Africa is old. Africa is rich. Africa is poor. One thing can be said for certain about Africa, there's always something new to see and discover. Some people consider Africa the most important continent in the world. This book will explain why that is so. For example, Africa is the birthplace of all humankind; it's the place where agriculture and money were invented, and where art, music, and culture first flourished. Africa contains the world's longest river, longest lake, and largest desert.

Kilimanjaro, the highest freestanding mountain in the world, with elephants in Amboseli (am-bow-SAY-lee) National Park.

The scenery of Africa is rich, varied, and often spectacular. Most of Africa comprises vast stretches of rolling savannas and grasslands. A valley called the Great Rift is thousands of miles long, a mile deep, and 50 miles across. There's a snow-capped mountain, Kilimanjaro (KI-lee-man-JA-ro), which is the tallest freestanding mountain in the world.

Africa is also rich in plant and animal life. It is home to large numbers of living things and a lot of different species. This combination of plants and animals of many different sorts is called "biological diversity," or "biodiversity" for short. The Cape region of South Africa and the island country of Madagascar (mad-ah-GAS-gar) in the Indian Ocean have more native species of plants than anywhere else in the world except the Amazon basin. Only the forests of the Amazon and Australia have as many mammals and birds as Africa. And Africa is the place where the largest land animal in the world, the elephant, still roams free. After driving two hours outside Kenya's capital city, a visitor can observe a herd of elephants at the foot of Kilimanjaro.

Although the natural wonders of Africa are an important part of this book, its aim is to show

Today's Africans.

North American kids that Africa is not a jungle full of wild animals and wandering tribes of hunter-gatherers. In fact, it's hardly a jungle at all, with less than one-tenth of its surface covered with forest. Africa's animals may be among the most exciting on earth, but so are its people, who are just as likely to be found sitting around a conference room in a modern office building as squatting around a camp-fire in the bush.

This book is divided into three sections: "The African Continent," "African Plants and Animals," and "African People and Places." Enjoy the safari.

Map of Africa

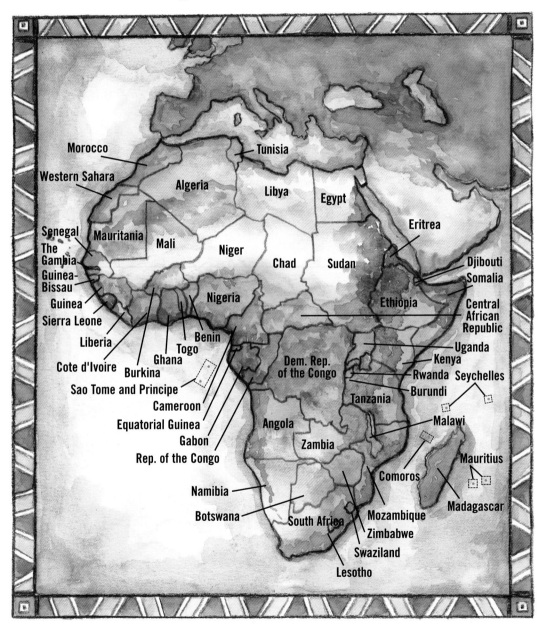

Morocco

Tunisia

Western Sahara

Algeria

Libya

Egypt

Eritrea

Senegal

The Gambia

Mauritania

Mali

Niger

Chad

Sudan

Djibouti

Somalia

Guinea-Bissau

Guinea

Nigeria

Ethiopia

Central African Republic

Sierra Leone

Benin

Uganda

Liberia

Togo

Kenya

Ghana

Dem. Rep. of the Congo

Rwanda

Seychelles

Cote d'Ivoire

Burkina

Burundi

Sao Tome and Principe

Tanzania

Cameroon

Malawi

Equatorial Guinea

Angola

Gabon

Zambia

Rep. of the Congo

Comoros

Mauritius

Namibia

Madagascar

Botswana

Mozambique

South Africa

Zimbabwe

Swaziland

Lesotho

Part One

The African Continent

The Vastness of Africa

Africa is huge. It is the second largest continent after Asia, and it takes up one-fifth of the land surface of the entire world. This fact is not always made obvious by maps. Most people are familiar with a world map based on the one made more than 500 years ago by Gerardus Mercator, a European mapmaker, for early explorers and their ship navigators. None of these Europeans knew very much about the world, and most of them rather selfishly thought that Europe and, after 1492, North America were the most important places on earth. So their maps projected a picture of the world that emphasized the northern hemisphere of the globe.

The Mercator map is the one still used in most classrooms around the world. However, while it is good for plotting courses across oceans, the Mercator map is terrible for estimating size. Africa looks only slightly larger than the United States. But take a look at a globe or an image taken from a satellite. Africa fills nearly a whole side of the globe. That's the trouble with maps of large areas that present a curved surface on a flat piece of paper.

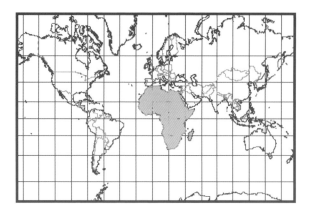

The Mercator map: a false impression.

Africa is huge.

There are some paper maps that display comparative area sizes better. Imagine making a map by peeling off the surface of the earth like the skin of an orange and laying it down flat on a page. Such a map is called an equal area projection because all of the continents and countries are shown in their true relation to one another. The big ones look big, the small ones, small.

The African continent is so big that three continental United States could fit into it.

Africa is the oldest continent. Most of the land has been in the same place for over 550 million years, and some of it since the beginning of life itself, 360 billion years ago. Does that mean the earth is a pretty stable chunk of rock? Not really. In fact, most of the surface of the earth is made up of a dozen gigantic slabs of rock called "tectonic plates" that are actually floating on the earth's softer, hotter center. Up until about 200 million years ago, all of these tectonic plates were clustered together into one large landmass called Pangaea (pan-GAY-ah).

The earth was very unstable back then, its surface heaving with great volcanic eruptions. Pangaea began to break into two pieces 180 million years ago. One, called Laurasia (lawr-AZE-ee-ah), floated north; the other, Gondwana (gone-DWAH-nah), stayed in the south. At this time Africa was attached to South America, but Antarctica had already begun to drift away to the south. The separation of South America, Africa, and Madagascar began some 115 million years later.

How do we know that the continental drift happened? First of all, geologists have found ancient rock formations in Brazil that are similar to some found in west Africa. Other formations in India, Australia, and Antarctica are like some found in East Africa and Madagascar. Second, a number of plant and animal species, both living and fossilized, can be found on more than one continent. It is unlikely that all of them crossed thousands of miles of ocean by accident. These similarities help prove that the continents were once, long ago, all attached. And finally, look at the shapes of the modern continents. If the clock were to run backward, it is easy to imagine how South America might fit into the southwestern kink of Africa and how Antarctica,

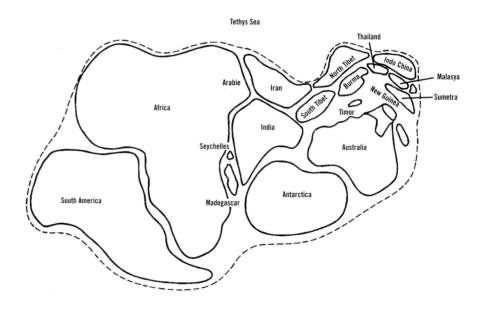

Madagascar, and India tuck neatly along Africa's eastern side.

While all these monstrous movements were taking place, Africa pretty well stayed put in the middle of things as the other chunks drifted away. Much of the southern half of Africa is where it was in the beginning. The Sand River rocks (technically called gneisses [g-NEE-ses]) of northern Transvaal (trahns-VAHL; roll the *r*) formed about 3.8 billion years ago and are nearly as old as the earth itself. Some of these formations are exposed, and there are places where you can have a picnic right on top of the oldest rocks in the world.

Despite its vast age, Africa is still changing, from drifting sands in the Sahara Desert to erupting volcanoes in the Great Rift Valley. What are the controlling factors of these movements, the things that determine the formation of the land?

Rock and Dirt: Geology and Soils

Every once in a while, even today, the earth produces signs that it has not finished forming. A city crumbles in an earthquake, a new island appears in the middle of the sea, or a volcano erupts on land. These sorts of events happened all the time when the earth was young, and they have been important ways for minerals to get from the earth's interior to its surface.

Most African soils are volcanic, meaning they were formed from rocks and ash that have been blasted out of volcanoes. These soils are particularly rich in minerals. Minerals trapped inside rocks are pretty useless as food for living beings. If they can get free, they can become food for plants and animals. Energy is needed to break down rocks, like the eroding energy of running water or the heating and cooling energy of the sun. Africa has had plenty of both over the earth's history, particularly in ancient times when even the Sahara Desert had plentiful rainfall.

Water makes the land. What does that mean? It means that millions and millions of years of rainfall and running water have worn down the rocks that make up the earth's surface and shaped the landscape. The rainfall that gathers in rivers gradually carves its way deeper into the rock and creates interesting topography. Just look at the Grand Canyon.

Minerals are freed from rocks through erosion. Erosion describes the movements of rock and dirt as water runs downhill. Erosion by water and wind over very long periods is called "weathering." Weathering exposes minerals at the earth's surface and then helps break them down into soil.

Depending on the steepness of the slope, the kind of soil, and the amount of vegetation, different amounts of water soak into the soil. After the water soaks into the soil, plant roots make good use of it. If the soil is porous, some of the water continues

Investigate Soil Erosion

Dirt plus water equals . . . a mess! Be sure to do this muddy activity outdoors.

Dirt is just dirt? Not so when it comes to soil erosion. Explore the ways different soils erode. You are going to "make it rain" over two or three slopes with different soil types to see which type is more susceptible to erosion.

Adult supervision required

You'll need

3 shallow boxes. The ideal size is 3 feet long by 2 feet wide by 4 inches deep, but anything close will do, as long as the boxes are shallow and can be sealed to hold soil.

Shovel

Trowel

3 different types of soil—enough to fill the boxes to ½ inch from the top. For example, humus-rich dirt dug up from under the leaf litter of a wooded plot or from under a big old shrub in a garden (get permission!); a clay soil like the yellowish stuff around a building site (clay soils tend to feel a bit slimy between the fingers when wet); a sandy soil (if you live near a sandy beach, most soil on the land side of the dunes will be sandy; otherwise, just use pure sand from a building site or a sandbox)

Scissors or Exacto knife

Access to outdoor stairs or a folding chair and a couple of pieces of wood or building blocks (choose materials that you don't mind getting wet)

3 large (quart size) jars or other large glass or clear plastic containers

A bathing suit or clothing you don't mind getting wet in

Garden hose with an adjustable spray nozzle. If a garden hose is not available, a watering can or a bucket of water poured through a large kitchen sieve will work

Stopwatch or watch with second hand

A willing assistant

Masking tape

Felt-tip pen or marker

Plastic bags

20–30 sticks, about 8 inches long

Repeat the steps below for each soil type. Treat each soil the same way. Make sure no soil type is wetter than the others and pack each down to the same density.

1. Fill one of the boxes with soil to about ½ inch from the top. Pack the soil lightly by slapping it down with the palm of your hand. Don't pack it too tightly. You should be able to easily stick your fingers through the dirt and touch the bottom of the box.

2. Carefully tear or cut out a narrow V-shaped piece about one-third of the way (1 to 1½ inches) down one corner of the box to create a "drain," so that water running over the soil will accumulate and exit from that corner.

3. Prop up the box on an angle. The easiest way is to lay it lengthwise across two stairs. Position the lower end on the second stair protruding over the edge so that a jar will fit under the corner of the box.

Another option is to use a chair and a block. Position the box so that the high end is elevated not less than one-third of its length. Jiggle the box's position so the "drain" is the lowest part of the box by one to two inches and the box protrudes enough to get a jar underneath.

4. Get the water gear together. If you have a hose with a nozzle, adjust it so that the hose produces a medium-to-coarse spray, just like raindrops in a good shower. If the hose does not have an adjustable nozzle, make an even spray by partially closing your thumb over the end of the hose. If you are using the bucket-and-sieve method, ask a friend to hold the sieve while you pour. Practice on the grass or pavement with any of the three methods until you are confident you can produce an even flow of water for about 20 to 30 seconds (as long as it takes to fill up the jar).

5. Place the jar under the "drain" and "make it rain" as evenly as possible over the soil. Keep making rain (even if you have to pause and fill up the bucket) until the jar is full.

6. Label the jar with the masking tape and felt-tip pen according to the soil type it drained: humus, clay, or sand, as appropriate.

7. Place the jar to one side and repeat the steps for each soil type.

8. Compare the water samples. Is there a difference in their turbidity (the cloudy quality of water produced by the soil sediment)? What can you conclude about which soil types are more vulnerable to erosion?

Since you have the materials set up and are already wet, you can also test the role of vegetation cover in controlling soil erosion.

You will need additional materials to simulate vegetation. Get some old plastic bags and 20 to 30 (depending on the size of your soil box) sticks about eight inches long. Cut the bags into 20 to 30 small, three-by-three-inch squares, and poke the stick through their middles to make little artificial trees.

Repeat the preparation in steps one through six above, using the soil type that showed the most loss from erosion. But this time, before you "make it rain," plant the little artificial trees so that they make a canopy that covers at least half the area of the soil bed.

Now compare the turbidity of the water samples with and without vegetation cover. Can you see a difference? Can you imagine how cutting down trees over thousands of square miles has affected Africa's soils?

Be sure to clean up the steps, chair, buckets, and jars after the experiment!

downward until it accumulates in aquifers or underground rivers.

In the dry areas of Africa, there is usually too little vegetation to break the fall of rain. During the wet season downpours, raindrops smash onto the bare soil, loosen the particles, and carry them off the land, along depressions, down little gullies, and into creeks, small rivers, big rivers, and at last the sea. Soil erosion is a huge problem in Africa and has been for a long time. The accumulation of silt at river mouths can be a mile thick.

Most of the minerals that crumble off the rocks pile up as young rocky soil. Then, slowly, sun and rain, heat and cold, natural acids made from water mixing with chemicals in the soil, and the roots of plants wriggle their way into the cracks in the rocks and the rocks crumble, mix with the organic debris, and eventually become soil.

Soil tends to display the characteristics of the parent rocks from which it came. Some soils, like those that come mainly from volcanoes, are very rich in minerals because they originated deep in the earth. Many volcanic soils in East Africa today are being washed into rivers and then into the sea at the rate of two to three inches per year. In 100 years, some places will have no soil left at all, only the underlying rock. Other soils, like the ones derived from granite rocks, are stony and poor in nutrients.

Over time, the chemical composition of soil may change as animals from earthworms to elephants add their dung to the soil. Soil can also move vast distances by the action of rivers. The Nile River carries soil along its 4,000-mile length, from the Ethiopian mountains and the East African highlands through Egypt to the Mediterranean Sea. As the river water flows into the sea, soil particles settle and produce a great mudflat—a delta—spreading out from the river's mouth. Because the soils of the Nile Delta were so fertile, agriculture flourished as long ago as 12,000 B.C. and became the basis of the ancient Egyptian civilization.

Climate: Seasons and Rainfall

Forget about the four seasons in Africa. Although there may be a few weeks of snow on the tops of the Atlas Mountains in Algeria in December or the Drakensberg (DRAH-kens-bairg) Range in South Africa in July, there are no winter or summer season in Africa as Americans and Europeans know them. And without winter and summer, there's no equivalent of spring or fall.

In Africa, there are basically two seasons: wet and dry. What's important is how much rain falls to the earth. Plentiful rainfall is required for agriculture, and therefore human economies and livelihoods ultimately depend on it. Even modern irrigation in deserts uses water from rain that fell elsewhere.

Most African countries, especially those in western and southern Africa north of the Limpopo (lim-

Typical cumulonimbus rain clouds dumping water over the East African savanna during the rainy season.

POE-poe) River, have one rainy season and one dry season. The northern part of Mali in west Africa, on the edge of the Sahara, gets only five inches of rain per year. Others, like the eastern African countries Kenya and Tanzania, are influenced by monsoons and may get 40 inches in two rainy seasons, with the wettest times in April and November. In the far north, in Tunisia (toon-EEZ-ee-ah), for example, and in the most southern region of South Africa, the climate is called "Mediterranean," with a cool, wet winter and long, hot summer. In the Congo, along the equator, it rains most of the year, a total of 80 inches, almost seven feet of rain!

The big difference between the rainfall in most African countries and most of the world is not so much the amount but the way it's distributed over the year. Washington, D.C., gets the same amount of rain in a year as Nairobi (nahee-ROW-bee), the capital of Kenya—a total of about 40 inches. Washington and Nairobi are both woody and green. But while Washington stays that way all year round (the grass even remains green under the snow in the winter), the grass in and around Nairobi dries up and may even burn in wildfires each year. The difference is that in Washington it rains a little bit at least once a month; in Nairobi, the rains come crashing down, mainly in April. Much of the water can't be absorbed by the soil and runs off into the Indian Ocean.

Modifying Forces

Water and sunlight are the earth's main modifying forces. The three "-tudes"—altitude, latitude, and attitude—help determine local conditions.

Altitude

Three important climate features change with increases in the altitude above sea level. It gets colder, there is less oxygen, and there is greater solar radiation. Air cools at a rate of about 5½ degrees for every 1,000 feet of height increase above sea level. So if it's about 95° F on the Tanzanian coast on the Indian Ocean, how cold will it be on the 19,330-foot top of Kilimanjaro? At night, it will be below zero. Nairobi, at 5,500 feet—about the same height as much of the Appalachian mountain range in the United States—is around 70°F, again at night with no sun. (Read on, before protesting that the tops of the Appalachians are much colder!)

Air gets "thinner" at higher altitudes. Above 10,000 feet, people begin to breathe heavily, and higher than 14,000 feet, neither plants nor humans have enough oxygen to survive happily. As the air thins, more ultraviolet radiation from the sun penetrates the atmosphere and burns human skin and plant tissue. People wear hats and sun-blocking cream; the plants on Mount Kenya, and the Mountains of the Moon in Uganda, grow smaller leaves with thick, waxy surfaces.

Latitude

Latitude is the measure of how far a place is north or south of the equator, from 0 degrees at the equator, up 90 degrees to the North Pole, or down 90 degrees to the South Pole.

The farther north or south from the equator, the steeper the angle of the sun's rays hitting the earth becomes. That's why the top of a 5,000-foot Appalachian peak is colder on average than Nairobi. The fact that the sun beats down directly on the humans who live on the equator contributed to the way early humans evolved in Africa (see page 65).

One of the most northerly cities in Africa, Tunis in Tunisia is at about the same latitude as Las Vegas or Nashville, and all three cities can get down to just above freezing on a cold winter night. Going by latitude alone, one would expect that Cape Town near Africa's southern tip would reach about the same temperatures as Los Angeles: both are about 2,300 miles from the equator (one south, the other north). In fact, Cape Town is a bit cooler because an ocean current from Antarctica cools the coastal water.

Attitude

Attitude refers to the tilt of the earth, which affects seasons, winds, and currents. Seasonal temperature shifts and rainfall are caused by one thing: the 23½-degree tilt of the earth's axis. This tilt puts the Northern Hemisphere slightly closer to the sun for six months (April to September) and then farther away for the next six (October to March).

Obviously, being closer to the sun makes the earth warmer; farther away, colder. South of the equator, the tilt has a similar effect, but for the opposite six months. The cold season is in July, and the hot season is at its peak in December. It never gets really cold throughout most of Africa, maybe just a few degrees above freezing on a clear night in the desert.

The area between the equator and the latitude 30 degrees north forms a band around the earth about 2,000 miles wide. In that band, winds tend to come from the northeast. In a similar band south of the equator, winds tend to come from the southeast. The northerly and southerly trade winds meet in the so-called Intertropical Convergence Zone (ITCZ). The annual shift of the ITCZ determines the annual pattern of winds and rainfall across Africa. Like a huge seasonal clock mechanism, the ITCZ and the trade winds affect both planting seasons and seafaring commerce. Why do the winds change course?

Because, on average, the earth is closest to the sun at the equator, the air around the earth's middle heats up and rises quickly. It bumps into the cool upper layers of the atmosphere and, before it can cool down, gets diverted toward the poles, both north and south. Not only that, it also gets pushed or pulled sideways because of the earth's spin.

A spy satellite hovering over the North Pole for a whole day would see the earth turning counterclockwise, which is why the sun appears to rise in the east and set in the west. The earth also tilts a few degrees on its axis throughout the year. In July, the top half

Monsoons

A monsoon is a wind system that seasonally reverses direction over a very large area, like one that blows for six months from the northeast and six months from the southwest over the Indian Ocean and the eastern African coast north of Madagascar. During the Northern Hemisphere's winter (November to April), high pressure over Asia and low pressure from latitude 10 degrees south all the way to Australia result in winds from the northeast: air is squeezed out of the high pressure area into the low.

For over 1,000 years, seafaring merchants from the Persian Gulf and the Arabian Peninsula have ridden the *kaskazi* (kas-KAZ-ee, meaning "east" in Swahili) winds to trade with Africa, bringing spices, cloth, china plates, metal tools, and utensils from the East. From May to October (the Northern Hemisphere's summer), low atmospheric pressure over Asia and high pressure over Australia reverse the monsoon winds so they come from the southwest. This is the *kusi* (KOO-see, meaning "south"), the 25-mile-per-hour winds that pushed the trading ships back home to the Arabian Peninsula, laden with ivory, gold, and slaves.

Rainy Seasons

These graphs compare the average monthly rainfall in Washington, D.C., with that of Bamako, the capital of Mali in west Africa, and Nairobi in East Africa. The Washington rainfall is pretty uniform throughout the year, typical of a Northern Hemisphere coastal city. The west Africa pattern is "unimodal" (you-knee-MOW-dal, meaning most of the data on a graph is piled up in one place, making one peak), with most of the rain falling July through September. It is difficult for North Americans to imagine going most of the year without a nice rain shower. East Africa is "bimodal" (BYE-mow-dal, meaning the graph displays two peaks of data), with two main wet periods, one in April and the other in November. All three cities get about the same amount of rain in a year, 40 inches, but notice how differently it falls.

Three cities with roughly the same rainfall but different rainy seasons.

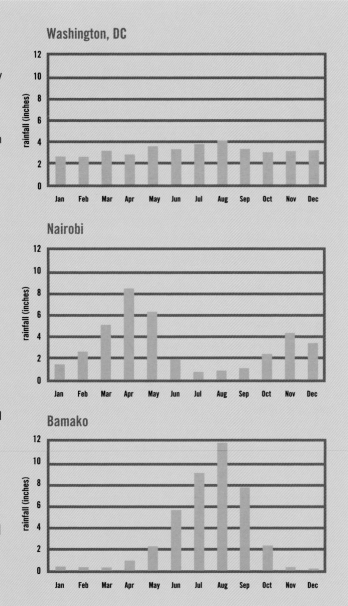

is closer to the sun and the bottom half is farther away. In January, it's the opposite. That's what makes winter in the earth's Northern Hemisphere.

Without the earth's spinning and tilting, its atmosphere would settle down and warm up nice and evenly all over—find a thermal equilibrium in technical terms. But the air is never still, the earth spins and tilts, and the sun rises and sets.

Winds and Currents

Although the earth's climate is complex, the wind patterns are quite regular. So regular, in fact, that people have used them to navigate along the same routes since the dawn of exploration and trade, which is why these reliable winds are called "trade winds." The trade winds had a big effect on the modern history of Africa.

Ocean currents, at least on the surface, move more or less according to the trade winds. The deep ocean currents also move with the rotation and gravitation of the earth, and, like air, they move up and down depending on temperature: warm water rises and cool water sinks. Deep ocean currents help control the earth's climate.

The water that flows from the open ocean greatly affects the temperature in coastal waters and indirectly affects the abundance of fish. This is because cold water usually comes from the deep ocean, where there is a rich accumulation of nutrients—lots of fish food. The currents also influence

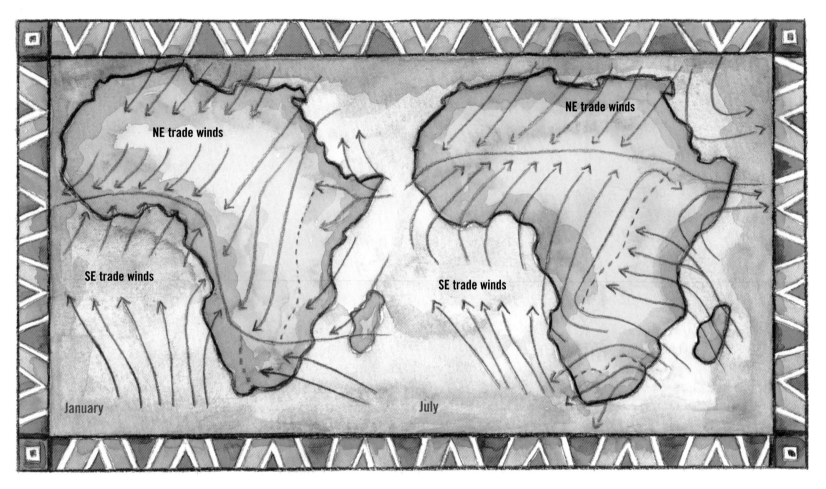

NE trade winds

SE trade winds

January

NE trade winds

SE trade winds

July

The Intertropical Convergence Zone is one of the places on the African continent where opposing wind currents meet.

——————— intertropical convergence zone

– – – – – other zones of convergence

———————▶ wind currents

11

The path of the Great Rift Valley in eastern Africa. The purple lines trace the main faults and cracks in the earth's surface. It's easy to conclude that the Horn of Africa may one day become an island.

the local climate on shore. The Atlantic West Wind Drift is a cold water current starting near Antarctica from below South America. It rises up on the continental shelf as it approaches South Africa and cools the southwestern coast. Old-time mariners would follow the current north as it became the Benguela (ben-goo-EH-la) Current along the Namibian (nah-MIB-ee-ahn) Desert. The current is so strong and there are so many rocks that hundreds of old sailing ships were wrecked there, which is why they call that stretch the Skeleton Coast.

The cold Canaries Current that wells up from deep waters off Europe improves fishing off the Moroccan coast. The hot South Equatorial Current flows westward in the Indian Ocean, bumps into Africa around Madagascar, and then splits to the south and north, which makes swimming along the eastern African coast like taking a warm bath.

But there is a lot of variation in temperature and rainfall across Africa because of the continent's vast size, which stretches from the hot equatorial region to cool temperate areas both north and south, and because of the cooling and wetting effects of three major water bodies: the Atlantic and Indian oceans to the west and east and the Mediterranean Sea to the north.

The East African Rift

Imagine a giant holding the earth like a basketball in the palm of his hand. Where on earth would he point to indicate the place where people first lived? He'd poke his finger into a crack between two separating tectonic plates in eastern Africa.

The East African Rift, as it is called, is one of the grandest features on the earth's surface. Astronauts easily spot it every time they orbit the earth (see the space view, left). It stretches 4,000 miles from Jordan in southwestern Asia southward through eastern Africa to Mozambique (mohz-ahm-BEEK). On average it's about 30 to 40 miles wide, an easy two-day walk for our early human ancestors.

The rift has two branches. The main branch, often called the Great Rift Valley, extends along the entire length of the rift. The rift is full of large and famous water bodies. In the north, the Middle East, it's occupied by the Jordan River and the Dead Sea. It carries on southward as the Red Sea, through Ethiopia into Kenya, where rainwater collects in lakes Turkana (toor-KHAN-ah), Naivasha (n'eye-VASH-ah), and Magadi (mah-GAHD-ee). Some of its cliffs are as high as 9,000 feet. In Tanzania the rift is less obvious because the eastern rim is very eroded. It wanders southward as the Shire River Valley and Mozambique Plain and ends up on the Indian Ocean coast in Mozambique.

The other branch is the Western Rift Valley, which extends northward from the northern end of Lake Malawi (mah-LAH-wee) in a great arc that contains the lakes Rukwa (ROOK-wah), Tanganyika (tahng-gahn-EE-kah), Kivu (KEE-voo), Edward, and Albert.

Together, Africa's nine Great Lakes equal just over half the area of the United States' five Great Lakes. Most of the lakes in the East African Rift are very deep, and the bottoms of some are below sea level. Lake Tanganyika, at 4,800 feet, is the deepest in Africa and the second deepest in the world.

The East African Rift has been getting deeper for some 30 million years as the tectonic plates of Africa and the Arabian Peninsula drift apart. It's still moving at about one-eighth of an inch per year. Madagascar, the largest island off Africa's east coast, drifted off on its own about 160 million years ago. In a million or so years, all of Africa east of the rift may become another huge island.

Rivers

The world's longest river, the Nile, meanders some 4,130 miles from Uganda and north to Egypt into the Mediterranean Sea. That's the distance from New York to San Francisco. It drains rainfall from an area as big as the United States.

The quest for the source of the Nile was the greatest geographical challenge since the discovery of America. The early explorers who tried to follow the

Major African rivers and lakes.

Island Mountains

Thousands of years of weathering on the earth's surface, a process that scrapes away softer volcanic rocks and soil, creates islands of hard granite rocks. Weathering leaves behind a fantastic pile of huge boulders, which, in Tanzania, is called an *inselberg* (IN-sell-bare-g), which means "island-mountain" in German—Tanzania was once a German colony). The same thing happens in South Africa, where it's called a *kopye* (COP-yeah, which means "little head" in Afrikaans (ah-free-KHAnzz; say the last syllable with a kind of buzz), a language spoken in South Africa). Even the exposed boulders continue to be weathered by rain and extreme changes in temperature, ranging from the hot midday sun to the surprisingly cold nights, particularly at high altitudes (see page 8).

An island mountain protruding from the Serengeti (SER-en-GHE-tee) Plain.

Nile upstream always got bogged down in the great swamp of the Sudd in (guess which country?) Sudan, got sick, or were chased off by indigenous peoples. It was only about 150 years ago that explorers decided to start upstream and look for the river's source by trekking inland from the Indian Ocean. That worked.

It turns out that the Nile actually starts in two places and flows out of two lakes. The White Nile begins in Lake Victoria in eastern Africa. The Blue Nile starts in Lake Tana in the Ethiopian highlands. The two rivers meet in Khartoum (car-TOOM), the capital of Sudan, and continue as one through 2,000 miles of pure desert to the Mediterranean Sea through the Nile Delta in Egypt. Along this stretch all life—plants, animals, and people—lives near the shores. Go more than a mile from shore, and there's nothing but rock and sand.

The Congo River follows a different kind of path than the desert-crossing Nile. The Congo flows for 2,900 miles through real Tarzan-type jungle, starting in Zambia (ZAHM-bee-ah) and ending up in the Atlantic Ocean. Together, the Nile and the Congo drain an area larger than the United States. Since there are so few roads in the Democratic Republic of Congo, boats on the river are the main means of transport in the country.

The Niger River runs 2,600 miles from its source in the Fouta Djallon (FOO-tah D'JAW-lone) highlands in Guinea to the Atlantic. The third largest river in Africa, it is longer than the Mississippi River by a few miles.

Lakes

The saying "all rivers run to the sea" is sometimes untrue in Africa. In southwest Africa, for example, the Cunene (koo-NEH-neh) River used to flow south from Angola into a large lake in northern Namibia. Suddenly, a couple thousand years ago, it changed course—nobody knows why—and headed into the Atlantic Ocean. The lake dried up and became the largest salt flat in Africa, called Etosha Pan (eye-TOE-sha). A pan is a flat depression in the landscape, often covered by a hard layer of salty soil.

Etosha Pan is 1,900 square miles, a bit bigger than the Great Salt Lake in Utah. It has hot springs and little hillocks of salty clay that animals come from miles around to lick. Etosha National Park surrounds the pan and contains one of the largest concentrations of wildlife species in the world: lions, elephants, rhinoceros, zebras, and a variety of antelopes and gazelles.

Rivers that do not evaporate in some low-lying, dry place or flow into the sea generally end up in lakes. There are many important lakes in Africa, most in the Great Rift Valley, as we have discussed. The biggest lake is Lake Victoria, named after the 19th-century English queen. It is 26,000 square miles, which makes it similar in size to one of North America's Great Lakes—a bit bigger than Lake Huron, a bit smaller than Lake Superior. The longest lake in the world is Lake Tanganyika, which is more than 400 miles long.

The lakes are vital sources of protein for the local people, who survive mainly on fish. The most crowded places in Africa, apart from the big cities, are the lakeshores. The crowding and lack of basic sanitation among poor populations causes much disease and illness through water pollution.

Imagine a drum full of a special fluid on which life depends. Along comes someone who uses it wastefully and dumps sewage, rubbish, and poisonous chemicals into it. The person would have to be crazy, right? Yet that's exactly what is happening to the world's water supply. The situation is even worse in many parts of Africa, where the drum is only one-quarter full of water to start.

Water means life. People can go without food for weeks, but after three or four days without water, they will die. It is estimated that over half of Africa will experience a water shortage by the year 2025.

Since February 1998, the residents of Adamawa State have been experiencing brown water running out of their taps. This is a common problem in many developing countries. It has led to the outbreak of cerebral meningitis [a disease of the nervous system] and hookworm [a bloodsucking parasite that gets into the bloodstream and lives in the intestine].

—Daniel Onyi Eboh, Nigerian 15-year-old

Lake Tanganyika: Proof of Global Warming?

There has been a lot of discussion about global warming recently. Is it just by chance that in the last few years we have had the hottest summers in 100 years? Or is the earth really getting steadily warmer because of air pollution and the greenhouse effect? Some people deny that there's any change at all. Well, fishermen around Lake Tanganyika agree that something terrible is really happening: they are starving because of climate change.

For thousands of years, thousands of people have lived by fishing small freshwater sardines out of the longest lake in the world. The fishing used to be very rich because the surface waters—where the fish feed and get caught—regularly mixed with the deep bottom waters, where all the nutrients accumulate from decaying algae and runoff from the land. But over the last 30 years, the number of fish caught has dropped by half.

Here's what happened. As in many places in the world these days, the temperature in the region around Lake Tanganyika has increased. As a result, the upper waters of the lake have also become warmer. Only by a couple of degrees, but that's enough to change the whole lake. The slightly warmer water near the surface now tends to stay put because it is less dense: warm water floats on cold water. Also, because the temperature is uniformly warm year round, there's less wind stirring and fewer waves rolling at the surface to mix the water layers. The nutrients stay deep down in the lake, and the fish species that lived close to the surface, in reach of fishermen's nets, die out. This change means that there are fewer fish and more hungry fishermen.

Has Kilimanjaro Shrunk?

For more than 100 years, the altitude of Uhuru (oo-HOO-roo, meaning "freedom" in Swahili) Peak, the highest point on Kilimanjaro, was thought to be 19,340 feet above sea level. But a team of geologists from Tanzania and Germany climbed the mountain in 2001 and took a lot of measurements with very fancy Global Positioning System (GPS) equipment. They measured the mountain to 19,330 feet. Why the 10-foot difference? Were the old measurements consistently inaccurate? Did the old-timers forget to subtract for the thickness of the ice on top? Has the mountain really shrunk? No one knows.

Volcanoes and Mountains

On the edges of separating tectonic plates, the land can become unstable. There are more earthquakes and more volcanoes at these places. Most of Africa's mountains have been formed by volcanic activity. A few, like Nyiragongo (NYEE-rah-GONG-go) in the Congo or Ol Donyo Lengai (ol-DON-yo len-GUY, meaning the "mountain of God" in the Maasai [ma-SIGH] language) are a few million years old and are still active. Ol Donyo Lengai last puffed ash over the Serengeti National Park in Tanzania in the late 1950s.

In January 2002, Nyiragongo blew its stack. Streams of molten lava poured into the city of Goma on the north shore of Lake Kivu in the Democratic Republic of the Congo. More than 100 people were killed, more than 12,000 homes were destroyed, and 300,000 people had to flee from the lava.

Most of the volcanoes in Africa, like the mountain ranges in west Africa, the Mountains of the Moon in Uganda, and Kilimanjaro in Tanzania, have been extinct since humans evolved. *Kilima* means "little mountain" in Swahili. This name is a Swahili joke, because Kilimanjaro is, in fact, the tallest mountain on the continent. By the way, real mountaineers never refer to "Mount Kilimanjaro." That's like saying "Mount Mount Njaro," which sounds silly in any language.

Kilimanjaro ranks as the 36th highest mountain in the world, but, as we discussed earlier, it is the highest freestanding mountain; that is, no other mountain rises so high from a flat plane below, from 4,000 feet at the base to 19,330 feet at the summit, a difference of nearly three miles.

Kilimanjaro is so tall that it has permanent glaciers on its top. During the rainy season, the mountaintop is frequently dusted with snow. People in Europe thought the early explorers were crazy when they came back with tales of having seen snow less than 100 miles from the equator. *Njaro*, an old Swahili word derived from Arabic, probably means "bright" and was a description of the white snow on the mountain.

The mountain is a good example of vegetation zoning. As air travels from sea level at the Indian Ocean coast inland and upward, it becomes thinner and cooler. At the same time, the temperature is above 90 degrees on the Kenya coast and close to the Kibo summit it's below zero, which is why there are permanent glaciers on the top. A climber who wants to ascend Kili starts down on the arid plains of Tsavo National Park at around 4,000 feet and moves gradually upward through small-holder farms and forest plantations into thick natural forest.

At above 9,000 feet, the forest thins out into bushy heather and tussock grass, which, at around 12,000 feet, becomes moorland, a type of land that is distinguished by rolling tussocks of short, spiky grasses. It's hard to believe, but the vegetation in African moorlands is much like the vegetation growing in the European Alps and the North American

Rockies. Above 14,000 feet it is too cold and dry for plants, and the rest of the way up a climber has to scale rocks or snow and ice to get to the roof of Africa.

Mineral Wealth

The ancient rocks of Africa are full of mineral wealth, including gold, chrome, platinum, diamonds, and other precious stones. Some of the wealth is said to be hidden in the legendary King Solomon's mines, which probably do not exist. In fact, Africa's recent history includes a gold rush to extract the mineral riches. More than half of all the gold mined during human history has come from the Kaapvaal (CAHP-vahl) in northern South Africa. Half of the world's diamonds came from southern Africa. Africa's diamonds are both a blessing and a curse. They bring money to Africa, yet they have been the cause of fighting and atrocities. And new jewels are being discovered in Africa all the time. Within the past 50 years prospectors discovered two previously unknown gemstones and named them Kenyaite and Tanzanite—guess where they were found?

Glaciers Disappearing

Over the past 200 years, the glaciers on Kilimanjaro, like all the world's mountain glaciers, have begun to rapidly melt away due to the global warming of the earth's atmosphere. Why is the atmosphere becoming warmer? In part, because natural climate fluctuations occur over thousands of years. But many scientists believe the warmer temperatures are due mainly to the greenhouse effect. The factories and machines from the industrial development of the last 150 years have belched pollutants into the atmosphere that act like the glass in a greenhouse and trap more and more heat from the sun in our lower atmosphere. Even though Africa began industrial development more recently, the effects of the warming, like our atmosphere, are global. What happens in Cleveland matters on Kilimanjaro.

Kibo summit on Kilimanjaro. Uhuru Peak, the highest point in Africa, is to the left, just above the Western Glacier. In the early 1990s, Kibo was completely covered with ice and snow. By 2000, the glaciers were nearly gone.

Part Two

African Habitats, Plants, and Animals

The Pyramid of Life: The Big Picture

Life may appear to be endlessly complicated, with millions of species of animals and even more species of plants. But, in fact, the underlying relationships are really quite simple. Plants grow in the soil with the help of water and sunlight; herbivores eat plants; carnivores eat herbivores; scavengers are omnivores and eat plants, herbivores, and carnivores; parasites eat everyone. And when all of them die, they all decompose back into the soil. All of this voracious eating results in what is called the "pyramid of life." Lots of plants are at the bottom, a good number of herbivores are in the middle, a few carnivores are at the top, and scavengers and parasites crawl around the whole lot.

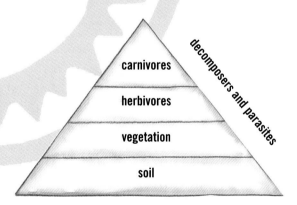

The pyramid of life: carnivores eat herbivores; herbivores eat vegetation; vegetation grows in soil; and decomposers and parasites eat them all!

Ecologists use the term "ecosystem" to describe the collection of plants and animals in a particular location, all fed by the energy of the sun and the nutrients from the soil. Within an ecosystem, all plants and animals on land are rained on from above by the same local weather and nourished by water from below by the same lakes, rivers, and underground springs.

One way of picturing an ecosystem and how it works is to imagine a tag attached to one atom of an element that makes up the basic building blocks of life, like carbon. Carbon is everywhere and is indispensable to life. Carbon atoms chain together and bond with other atoms to make all of the organic chemicals of life itself, from DNA to toenails.

So imagine that there is a traceable tag on a carbon atom that was blown out of Ol Donyo Lengai, the last active volcano in East Africa, when it last erupted in 1957. The atom is blown by the prevailing wind to the west, where it mingles with a rainstorm and is deposited as a dissolved salt into the soils of the famous Serengeti Plain in Tanzania.

Grass grows so fast in the African sun just after the rainy season that you can almost see it grow, half an inch a day. So it does not take long for the tagged carbon atom to be absorbed by a grass root and become part of the cell wall in a leaf. If it is the time of the great Serengeti migration, when a million wildebeests and thousands of gazelles and zebras trek across the plains and through the woodlands looking for fresh grass, there is a good chance that a passing

Observe a Local Ecosystem

Ecosystems are everywhere. See if you can observe what's happening in one near you.

In this activity, you will go to your backyard or the nearest woods, pond, or park and make a list of the species of plants and animals you see. The list should be based on the plant or animal's trophic level. "Trophic" comes from the ancient Greek word meaning "nourishment," and it refers to the relative placement of an organism on a food chain in terms of what it eats and who eats it.

You'll need

Pencil

Paper

Clipboard

Binoculars

Field guides to mammals, birds, and plants

1. Draw a large pyramid of life like the one shown on page 20, and label the compartments according to the major trophic levels. At the bottom there are producers. (Primary producers are almost always plants. We'll ignore organisms like bacteria for now, since you won't see them anyway.) Everything else is a consumer. The second trophic level comprises herbivores, and the top level contains carnivores. Along one side of the pyramid you'll have a space for decomposers and on the other for omnivores ("omni" means "all" or "everything" in Latin). Guess what they eat?

2. Spend a couple of hours (take a friend to help you spot things) wandering around or sitting quietly at one or two places at your chosen site, watching and writing down the species you see.

   A couple of tips: There are likely to be more plants than you can name, so just identify what you can with descriptions: write "oak tree," "little bush with red berries," "grass A," "grass B"—that sort of thing. Use your field guides to identify the species later. Keep going until you fill up the primary production box. If you don't know whether an animal is a herbivore or a carnivore, just make a note in the margin of your paper and try to identify it later by looking it up in your field guide or by asking your science or biology teacher. If you don't see a particular animal on the day of your survey but you know it lives in the ecosystem because you have seen it before, put it on the list.

You probably won't see too many omnivores unless you want to include people in your list, which is fine: we are important consumers in an ecosystem.

Decomposers are tricky, since they are often very small (like bacteria) and live in the soil or on unpleasant materials animals leave around the ecosystem. Decomposers like earthworms and flies are bound to be in most ecosystems.

3. When your list is complete (or as complete as the spaces in your trophic level diagram allows), draw the feeding relationships between organisms. For example, when a squirrel eats an acorn, materials and energy move from the oak tree in the producers trophic level to the squirrel in the herbivore level. The arrow goes up. Similarly, a cat would be happy to eat a squirrel, making another upward arrow from herbivore to carnivore.

Each animal is likely to eat a number of different things. The cat arrow might point to a sparrow (herbivore), hawk (carnivore—which eats, among other things, earthworms, which are decomposers), or crow (omnivore). In addition to acorns, the squirrel might eat seeds and berries.

4. At the end of this part of the activity, you should have an orderly mess of names and arrows that will become the food web of your ecosystem. Do any arrows point downward? If so, think again.

5. Ask yourself, what are the imports to and exports from the system? You could, for example, draw an arrow going from the earthworm right out of your ecosystem pyramid if you know fishermen dig them up for bait and carry them off to a nearby lake. Or if there is a field of corn in your ecosystem, you could draw a big arrow out at harvest time. Imports might include the fertilizer the farmer puts on the fields each year or the peanuts you bring into the park to feed the squirrels. Very few ecosystems are islands (except islands).

wildebeest will eat the leaf. The carbon atom is among many others that get chewed, swallowed, and digested by a wildebeest and become a part of the animal.

Life then gets exciting for the atom. The wildebeest is cut off from its herd and run down by a pack of African wild dogs. The wild dog, with its colorful blotches and big ears, looks harmless, even comical. It is also much smaller than a wildebeest, smaller even than a German shepherd. But wild dogs hunting in a pack can attack and tear apart a wildebeest in a matter of minutes.

So the dogs eat the wildebeest, but the chunk of meat with the carbon atom in it is stolen by a jackal, who is chased off by a large vulture, who gulps down the meat before the jackal can retaliate. In a few hours the vulture leaves some droppings containing the carbon atom a few miles away. A soil bacterium absorbs the atom and excretes it back into the soil as an organic molecule or an inorganic salt. It is not long before another plant takes up the atom, and off it goes again on the big merry-go-round of life.

Chances are that over the following years the tagged carbon atom would see far more of the Serengeti National Park than any tourist. It could become a part of the grasses and bushes that are eaten by herbivores like impalas, giraffes, and locusts, animals and insects that are preyed upon by carnivores like lions, cheetahs, and birds of prey. The atom is then recycled by decomposers like vultures and worms, then—plop—back into the soil, ready to run through the system once more.

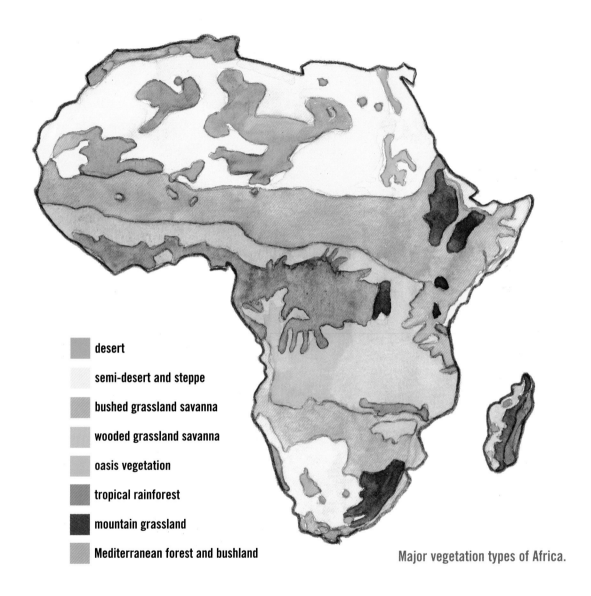

desert

semi-desert and steppe

bushed grassland savanna

wooded grassland savanna

oasis vegetation

tropical rainforest

mountain grassland

Mediterranean forest and bushland

Major vegetation types of Africa.

Ecologists call the route from vegetation to herbivore to carnivore to decomposer a "food chain." Over the years the atom could have traveled through all the possible food chains in the neighborhood, even the whole food web of the Serengeti ecosystem. That's what happens in an ecosystem. After years of cycling around from the soil through different plants and animals and back to the soil again, the atom finds itself not very far from where our wildebeest first ate it—probably not more than 50 miles away, maybe less. It might even end up in an aquatic ecosystem, feeding the fish and fishermen of Lake Victoria.

Every ecosystem has its own special characteristics. It has, for example, a geographical location. The boundaries of the ecosystem often coincide with a number of physical boundaries, like a rift valley wall or a lakeshore or the boundary between two soil types. Each ecosystem usually includes a certain type of vegetation, like the forests and grasslands described in the following section.

Vegetation Types

African ecosystems include just about every kind of vegetation that exists, from mountain moorlands to coastal mangrove swamps. In the "Pyramid of Life," the physical features of a particular area—like soil, topography, and climate—are the forces driving the production of a particular kind of vegetation. The language used to describe vegetation depends on the structure of the plant communities; that is, what plant species are included among the local vegetation and the way the species grow as grasses, weeds, bushes, or trees.

Plant communities in Africa include tropical rainforests, tropical deciduous forests, bushlands, savanna grasslands, desert shrubs, and mountain vegetation. Climate largely determines the type of vegetation that grows in a region. Big trees are not found in a desert (except palm trees around an oasis), because trees need a lot of water to grow.

The word "habitat" describes the place where a certain organism lives, be it a plant and bacterium, or an animal like an elephant, crayfish, or kid. A habitat can be quite complicated to describe because it's made up of all the physical features of the land (soil type, altitude, latitude, incline, windiness, and average rainfall) and the vegetation type found in a particular place.

The sections that follow provide a quick tour of the major habitats of Africa, discussing the vegetation and introducing a few of the interesting people and animals that live in these special African environments.

Forests

Contrary to many popular depictions, Africa is not one big jungle, like the one in which Tarzan swings from tree to tree in movies. The amount of jungle, which is more properly called tropical (closed-canopy) rainforest, covers less than one-tenth of the

Deforestation

Deforestation is a big problem in Africa. Forests are disappearing at a frightening rate. There are two main reasons: one has to do with the behavior of poor people, the other with the behavior of rich people.

A poor man is trying to grow crops on a tiny plot of land with bad soil. It is the middle of a drought. His maize crop has resulted in two miserable cans of corn. He has no money to buy food to feed his hungry family. In the forest up the mountain there are still many trees growing. If he could cut down just one, he could make some charcoal to sell at the roadside (people use charcoal in the local town for cooking). He would then have a little money to buy enough food for the next couple of weeks and a bit of charcoal left for his family's fire. What to do?

Deforestation.

The other kind of deforestation starts with the demands of rich people. They are able to afford nice things such as, for example, a coffee table made from mahogany, a tropical forest hardwood that is protected by law in most places. The high price of the luxurious coffee table encourages a whole line of suppliers—furniture makers, lumber yards, timber importers, timber exporters, and lumberjacks—to work extra hard to produce it. The poor lumberjack, like the charcoal maker in the first example, is more concerned with feeding his family than protecting mahogany trees. He is driven to break the law in order to make some money.

Westerners with full bellies and good social services rush to protect the trees. They argue—correctly—that in the long run the trees will protect the soil, help capture raindrops, conserve water, and provide habitats for mammals, birds, and insects. But poor Africans have to feed their families now, today. They have no choice. The governments in certain countries are corrupt and give them no alternatives. So they sneak into the forest and chop down trees.

Multiply such stories by thousands, and it's clear why Africa's forests are quickly disappearing.

continent, mainly in central and western Africa along the equator and in west and East Africa along the coast. Because closed forests need a lot of water, small patches are found throughout Africa, particularly along rivers and at the edge of swamps. In total, African forests cover an area about the size of Alaska and Texas combined.

Thirty thousand years ago, the climate was cooler and wetter, and forests covered most of equatorial Africa. Today, Africa's isolated forests are sometimes separated by hundreds of miles and share many of the same species of plants and animals. The climate became drier between 25,000 and 12,000 years ago, and this caused the disappearance of much of the East African forests. That long dry spell also explains why these forests have fewer plant and animal species than, say, the Amazon in South America.

Of course, people have also had a hand in forest disappearance. Almost anywhere you go in an African forest, even one that looks totally untouched, you will find bits of charcoal, which shows that both fire and people have been there before.

Because forests support rich vegetation, they are very attractive to farmers. Forest soils are indeed very, very fertile as long as the minerals and water used by the trees are recycled. In other words, forest soils are fertile as long as there are forests. But the poor farmers feel that they have no choice but to cut down trees, make and sell charcoal, burn off the remaining bush, and plant crops.

Tropical forest: tall trees, many species, multiple layers.

When the trees are gone, the soil is next. It sometimes takes just one season's heavy rains pounding down directly on the soil to affect the forest for generations to come. The nutrients that dissolve in water are quickly washed away. The next dry season produces a brick-hard layer on top of the soil formed by a chemical reaction of metals in the soil (baked oxides of aluminum and iron). The sterile land could take 1,000 years to recover its nutrients.

My parents told me the forest is sacred. In the past, trees were cut responsibly, not indiscriminately for money, as they are today.

—Chris Ugwa, Nigerian 14-year-old

Trees cover the soil and enrich it with fallen decaying leaves; they also help conserve water. The leaves break the fall of raindrops and help them drip gently into the soil. Most rainwater is used where it falls in a forest. The canopy of leaves above keeps out the sun and slows the evaporation of moisture.

Trees may even help make rain. How? Both living and dead leaves give off tiny particles, kind of like plant droppings. These particles float into the upper layers of air and get swept up into clouds, tens of thousands of feet high. Water vapor in the tops of clouds freezes around the particles. The little blobs of ice grow heavy and fall back to earth. They warm up as they get lower and become rain. Forests may increase a region's rainfall by actually "seeding" the clouds above them. Seeding is the name of the process used to make clouds produce rain. Airplanes fly over clouds and dump crystals of a chemical such as sodium iodide or dry ice onto the clouds, which is a process similar to tossing seeds onto a plowed field. Ice forms around the particles and down they fall.

So removing forest cover not only wipes out valuable plants and animals and ruins the soil, it may also reduce the rainfall of the whole region.

Forest Animals: The Okapi

The forest is the habitat of many exotic animals, like the okapi (OH-kah-pee). Not only does the okapi look strange to a North American, it behaves strangely and can clean its eyes with its tongue. It has a foot-long, blue-black tongue that's perfect for stripping leaves off branches when it's not cleaning its eyes. It's a close relative of the giraffe, which also has a foot-long tongue. The okapi is quite large, about 500 pounds, with a stretched neck and dark red-brown fur. It has striking white stripes on its haunches and coloration that looks like it wears white knee socks. Despite its size, the strange coloration keeps the okapi camouflaged between the shadows and spots of sunlight on the forest floor.

European scientists first observed the okapi in 1901. Of course, the Mbuti pygmies knew about them much earlier. The animals are so shy and secretive that very little is known about their lifestyle—except by the Mbutis, but they don't usually write books.

Our Endangered Cousins

Human history includes many ugly episodes. When the Portuguese explorer Vasco da Gama anchored his ships on the Kenyan coast in 1497 to ask for directions, his soldiers chopped off the arms and legs of Swahili women to get their gold jewelry. More recently, less than 150 years ago, cruel and selfish men killed helpless members of tribes in the Amazon jungle, the Congo rainforest, and, yes, even in North and South America. Indigenous peoples were killed for their gold, timber, or land, or just for "fun," by prospectors, land grabbers, mining and timber companies, or the government militia. Today, most people condemn such barbaric behavior, and

The okapi: the giraffe's relative and the Ituri pygmy's neighbor.

Giant Grass

All through the forests, it is common to find large clumps of bamboo. On some African mountains, like the Mountains of the Moon (also called the Ruwenzori [ruin-ZO-ree]) on the Uganda-Burundi (yew-GAN-dah boor-OON-dee) border or Mount Kenya, bamboo grows in a zone between the elevations of 7,000 and 10,000 feet. Bamboo is really just a giant and ancient form of grass. Look closely at the structure of grass in a meadow: hollow, woody stems; long, flat leaves with parallel veins—just like bamboo. Bamboo also behaves like some annual grasses that mature in just one season, die off over the winter (or dry season), and grow again from seed when the temperature becomes warm and the earth becomes wet. Bamboo, too, only flowers once in its lifetime, but that may be as long as 90 years.

There are more than 1,200 species of bamboo around the world, and nearly half of them are in danger of extinction because forests are being cleared for agriculture and bamboo is being harvested as a fuel or building material. In Africa, bamboo loss also threatens species like the mountain gorilla, which depends heavily on bamboo for food in some seasons. In Madagascar, bamboo stands are important habitats for the very rare golden bamboo lemur (an ancient form of monkey) and the ploughshare tortoise, which is the rarest tortoise in the world. The food supply of both of these rare beasts in being chopped down and burned into oblivion.

Troop of Sykes monkeys wanders through a bamboo patch.

most countries have laws to protect all their citizens. Unfortunately, in some parts of Africa and other parts of the world, atrocities are still committed against ethnic groups.

If human rights organizations are still struggling hard to end violence against human beings, you can imagine how badly animals are being treated in many countries, African ones included. What do you think about people killing gorillas and chimpanzees, creatures that share more than 99 percent of their genes with humans? Chimpanzees are considered intelligent for many reasons. For example, unlike most animals, when a chimp looks in a mirror it knows that it is looking at itself. Chimpanzees regularly make and use tools. They can learn human sign language and make up simple words of their own when living with humans. They can be kind to their neighbors (they can be pretty vicious, too, just like humans). And, like humans, chimps have a long childhood that allows them to learn as much as they can from their mothers.

Some people shoot mother gorillas so they can sell the babies to people who want them as pets. Others kill chimpanzees and sell their flesh as bush meat in village markets. These practices are seriously threatening the future existence of these intelligent animals. These practices may also have threatened human existence. Some scientists believe that serious diseases like HIV/AIDS and Ebola have spread from apes to humans as humans consumed tainted bush meat.

Make a Zuna Wind Chime

If you're unsure how to tie the knots mentioned here, visit a knot-tying Web site, such as www.realknots.com, for assistance.

In most cultures, singing is an important way to express emotion or communicate with spirits or deities. A wind chime can be used to accompany a song or chant to keep evil spirits at bay or to attract good luck. The Zuna (meaning "abundance" in the Bobangi language of Nigeria) wind chime is made from bamboo, a material common in the highlands of most sub-Saharan African countries. Make your own wind chime, hang it in a breezy place, and enjoy its song all the time.

Adult supervision required

You'll need

Saw

6-foot length of bamboo, about 1 inch in diameter (available at a large garden shop)

Wood file

Pocketknife

6-inch nail

Hammer

Coconut

Hand drill with a ⅛-inch bit

10 feet of strong cord (string)

Scissors

1. Saw the bamboo into five lengths by cutting three-quarters of an inch above each node (the thick, hard, knoblike bump between each section of the bamboo). These will be your five chimes—hollow at one end and closed by the node at the other end. Cut the lengths slightly unequal to create a variety of sounds.

2. After cutting the five pieces, there should be some bamboo left with at least one spare node. Choose the biggest node and saw away the bamboo around it, leaving only the solid node. Use the file to smooth the edges. This will become the clapper of the wind chime. (If there's not a good node left, use a round piece of scrap wood about 1¼ to 1½ inches in diameter and ½ to ⅝ inch thick.)

3. With your pocketknife, carefully whittle away one side of the bottom one-half to one-third of the open end of each of the five bamboo lengths. Use the file to smooth the edges (careful, they're sharp!) of the bamboo lengths, creating a piece in the shape as shown below.

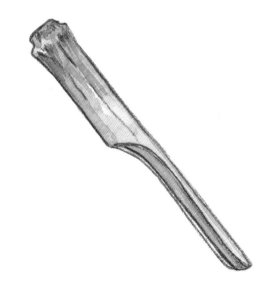

4. You'll need a break by now, so hammer two holes into the "eyes" of the coconut using the 6-inch nail, pour out the milk into a glass, and drink it. Then, saw off the top of the coconut (the part with eyes) about one-third of the way down to give you a cap for the wind chime about 3½ to 4 inches in diameter. Then saw off the bottom of the coconut to make a wind catcher about two inches in diameter. Chip out the coconut meat and put it aside.

5. Drill the following holes: one in the center of the clapper, six in the cap (you may be able to make use of the two "eye holes" if they are in the right place; otherwise, make new ones), one in the edge of the wind catcher, and one through the node of each chime.

6. String all the pieces together with the cord. This can be done in three stages.

   First, thread the chimes to the cap. Cut five lengths of cord about six inches long. Thread them through the holes in the chimes' nodes from the top. Tie a figure-eight knot in the chime end of each cord. Pull the knots up tight against the inside of the node. Thread the free ends up through the cap and tie a figure-eight knot to leave each chime

hanging two to three inches from the cap. Trim off the excess cord.

Next, to hang the clapper and wind catcher, cut a five-foot length of cord. Tie a figure-eight knot in the middle. Pass one end of the cord up through the center hole in the cap so that the knot ends up on the concave (rounded inward) side of the cap. Slide the clapper up the cord until it's about seven inches from the cap (it should be in position to strike the chimes just below where you have whittled them away). Tie another figure-eight knot to keep the clapper from sliding back down.

Finally, thread the cord through the hole in the wind catcher and tie a third figure-eight knot, so that the wind catcher hangs sideways about six to eight inches below the bottom of the chimes. Clip off the excess cord.

7. Pound the nail into a tree branch or, with permission, the corner of an eave on the porch, or a windowsill—any windy place—and hang the finished wind chime by its cord. Eat the coconut meat while enjoying the relaxing sound.

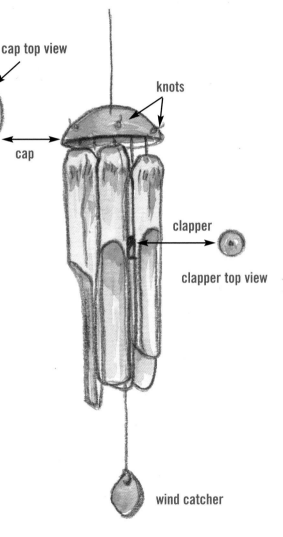

cap top view

knots

cap

clapper

clapper top view

wind catcher

Pygmy Culture in the Rainforest

Deep in the Congo, in a region called Ituri (ee-TOO-ree), bands of Mbuti (mm-BOO-tee) pygmies still follow an ancient lifestyle of hunting and gathering. They are small of stature, slightly built, quick and agile and well at home in a tangled forest environment. Because they share a habitat and sources of food with chimpanzees, there are many similarities between the groups' social behaviors (not too surprising considering that chimps and humans have more than 99 percent of their genes in common). For example, when food is abundant, both chimps and the Mbutis cooperate, socialize, and engage in enjoyable behaviors more often within their own communities. When food is scarce, however, individuals start behaving selfishly and try to keep food exclusively for themselves and their offspring. But there's a really big difference between chimps and people. When the going gets tough and fights are about to break out over food, people will talk and negotiate, though they may also argue and shout, whereas chimps will usually just fight.

The Mbutis are in big trouble. The same ruthless invaders to the forest that are killing chimps for "bush meat" are stealing the land and cutting down the forest that is the source of livelihood for the pygmies.

The gorilla is the largest living primate and the biggest ape. An adult male can weigh 400 pounds. Most primates are monkeys. Apes are tail-less monkeys. Writers and readers of books are primates, and, if most people weren't so proud, they would admit that humans are just very well developed apes and the close relatives of gorillas and chimpanzees, and gibbons, who live in South America, and orangutans, who live in Asia.

The gorilla, a gentle, leaf-eating giant, seriously threatened by hungry humans.

after an animal is killed, it's every chimp for him- or herself.

In contrast, gorillas are rather placid, and the huge silverback male—he has striking light-colored hair down his back—only makes his awesome chest-thumping display if another male tries to lure one of the females away from his small group. In the few places like the Bwindi (BWIN-dee) forest in Uganda where local people have agreed to protect gorillas and their habitats, the animals are so accustomed to people that tourists can get within a couple of yards of a group of gorillas placidly munching on leaves, their main food.

Chimps, particularly the females, make tools. They eat mainly fruit and fashion tools to open the hard shells of certain fruits. They use sticks or rocks to smash open a troublesome shell on a flat platform stone that may have been used by so many genera- tions of chimps that it has a hollow worn into its center. Chimps also carefully select and prepare thin sticks or grass stems to catch termites and ants in their holes. They make sponges out of chewed bark or leaves to soak up water in places that are hard to reach, and they can suck on the bark or leaves for a drink. They use soft leaves as rags and choose stiff, long ones to whisk off flies and to keep biting insects from landing on them.

Deserts and Arid Lands

Deserts are said to be deserted—abandoned by liv- ing things because they lack water. In fact, only in

The chimpanzee, a close relative in need of help.

Both gorillas and chimps live in their own extended family groups with much social inter- action. Chimpanzees are more aggressive than gorillas. Male chimps form gangs and patrol the borders of their clan areas, threatening and beat- ing up strangers. Chimps will also hunt down and kill monkeys, bush pigs, and small antelopes. They cooperate during a hunt, but

Noble Nomads

On the southwestern edge of the Sahara live the Tuareg (too-ARE-reg) people, a million strong, who some people say are descendents of one of the lost tribes of Israel. They are renowned warriors who tower menacingly in long flowing robes of deep blue on the backs of pale camels.

The Tuareg society is organized similarly to European society during the Middle Ages. There are lords and ladies, servants, clergymen, and a class of skilled artisans who make essential utensils, including weapons like their famous two-edge swords. They use a unique form of writing called *tifinagh* (tea-FIN-agh, which literally means "characters"). The language comes from an ancient Libyan script used in Roman times and consists only of consonants written from right to left.

Camels are their main livestock. On festive occasions, they hold wild camel races across sandy flats. The winner is surrounded by gleeful well-wishers firing their rifles into the air.

Tuareg women are considered to be among the most beautiful in Africa, but they must not be admired too openly or else an angry father, brother, or husband will draw his sword to run the admirer through.

The Tuaregs arrive at a wedding on the edge of the desert.

The Sahara desert.

certain parts of Africa's two great deserts—the Sahara in the north and the Namib (nah-MIB) in the southwest—support no life at all. Only one-fifth of the Sahara is pure sand, but that's a lot of sand, some 700,000 square miles, just bigger than Texas. In the rest of those and in the other smaller deserts—the Kalahari in Botswana (bots-WAH-nah) or the rift valley deserts like the Chalbe (CHAL-bee) in northern Kenya and the Danakil (DAN-ah-kill) in Ethiopia—often more living plants, animals, and insects appear when it rains. Even in the driest of deserts it rains sometimes—maybe less than an inch a year or only once every few years.

The Sahara Desert is known as the "mother of all deserts." It stretches 4,000 miles from the Red Sea in the east to the Atlantic Ocean in the west. It's over 3½ million square miles, as big as the continental United States. It wasn't always a desert. Millions of years ago, the area now called the Sahara Desert was covered with shallow seas, which left salt deposits that are mined even today. And as recently as 2,000 years ago, Roman legions harvested trees and caught elephants in what is now the Sahara.

But climates change, and when vegetation disappears because of decreasing rainfall, it is usually difficult to recover. Without vegetation cover, the earth's surface reflects more heat back into the atmosphere. That discourages clouds from forming, so even less rain falls. After a few hundred years, the land becomes a desert. This is another reason why it is so important to protect forests.

The Namib Desert is smaller, only 54,000 square miles, about the size of the state of Wisconsin. But it has two claims to fame: it is the oldest desert on earth, and it is the driest. Old, because it was part of the ancient land formations stretching back to Gondwana. Dry, because when the cold Benguela Current from the Antarctic Ocean hits the continental shelf, it pushes up cold air masses that dump all their rain into the sea before the winds hit the Skeleton Coast.

The Kalahari Desert, which covers much of northern Botswana, is 500,000 square miles, about the size of Alaska. The desert is indeed sandy, 650 feet deep in some places. Water soaks quickly through the ground, so most of the year there is very little moisture on the surface. Only the ingenious San Bushmen know how to survive there. But when it rains, nearly 10 inches every year, the Kalahari is alive with wildflowers, insects, birds, and small mammals.

The Danakil Desert is a ferocious place. Much of it is nearly 400 feet below sea level (Death Valley in Utah is only 280 feet below sea level), so it is exceedingly hot. It is the northern part of the Great Rift Valley before it becomes the Red Sea. But the main threats to life there are not natural ones. The rebel soldiers who cross through this desert are leftovers from the 30-year war between Eritrea (err-it-RAY-yah) and Ethiopia. As if that were not enough, a particularly fierce tribe of nomads, the Afar, frequent the Danakil as well.

Desert Adapted

The oryx (OH-ricks) is not a great runner. It lives in desert and semiarid habitats, where it's more advantageous to stop and turn a pair of long sharp horns toward a charging lion than become overheated and exhausted by running away. The oryx is the only herbivore of its size that has been known to kill a lion with its horns.

The impressive weapons of the oryx developed as an indirect adaptation to conserve water. Most herbivores rely on running to escape predators. Running generates sweat, which is then lost through evaporation. This process uses up precious body water reserves. Water loss is dangerous for an animal like the oryx. So, to get water, the oryx does much of its feeding at three o'clock in the morning, when the withered vegetation has absorbed a little moisture from the cool night air.

In the super-dry Namibian desert, the gemsbok (KHEMS-bock), the oryx's southern cousin, goes for

Why the Hippo Scatters Its Dung

San Bushmen in the Kalahari Desert spend long hours telling stories to their children and each other. Many of the stories involve the animals that they encounter on a daily basis and typically the storytellers account for some particular characteristic of the animal in question, in this case, why the hippo scatters its dung in all directions with its tail as it defecates. The San who live near the Okavango (OH-kah-VAHN-go) Delta in Botswana tell this story. (To read the story like a San elder, you'll need to click your tongue on the roof of your mouth wherever you see an exclamation mark; see section 3, page 104.)

Long ago, the Great God !Ga!ona ([click]-gah-[click]-OH-nah) was assigning to each animal its proper habitat in the world. A pair of hippos begged to be allowed to live in the cool water in which they loved to spend the day.

Now, !Ga!ona looked carefully at the hippos and was in great doubt about letting them stay in the water. They had huge mouths and big appetites, and he was concerned that they would eat up all the fish. Moreover, he had already let another large creature, the crocodile, live in the lakes and rivers. Two large fish eaters would simply be too much.

So, !Ga!ona refused the hippos' request and decreed that they should live out in the open grasslands.

The hippos began to weep and wail when they heard his decision. They made such a racket that !Ga!ona relented and offered them a compromise. They could stay in the rivers, but they must never eat fish. They had to eat grass, even if it meant grazing all night to avoid the hot sun.

The hippos agreed quickly, and with hardly a "thank you" they began to dash back to the river. !Ga!ona stopped them in their tracks and said, "And just to make certain that you follow my orders, I command you always to scatter your dung on the riverbank so that I may be certain it contains no fish bones."

To this day, hippos always scatter their dung on the riverbank. During the daytime you can hear the "Hu-uh, huh, huh, huh . . ." of their laughter as they rejoice in how lucky they are compared to the other grass eaters who must spend the day in the hot sun.

weeks without drinking and conserves water by not sweating. The gemsbok protects its brain from overheating through a special system of blood vessels between the nose and the base of the brain. The relatively cool blood that drains from inside the nose lowers the temperature of the blood coming from the heart by several degrees before it enters the brain. The gemsbok thus avoids thermal shock and brain damage in the heat of day when its body temperature, normally around 102°F, can exceed 120°F, near fatal for most mammals.

So long horns can help solve the overheating problems that are particularly acute in the desert, but this fierce weaponry also increases the risk of injury to other oryx in the group, some of whom may be related. This is probably why the oryx has such a striking black-and-white facial coloration. It's a social signal that means "a head sporting dangerous weapons is now turned toward you—beware!" And just in case a sparring match with another male gets out of hand, the skin of the oryx is a quarter of an inch thick on the neck and shoulders to help reduce damage from the horns.

Lakes and Rivers

Most people in North America, except those in the dry Southwest, live relatively close to a lake, river, or creek. Those who live in the Southwest know what it's like to live in more than half of Africa, where rivers run seasonally; that is, they only run during the rainy season. For most rural Africans, running water and lakes are rare and wonderful things.

The scimitar-horned oryx, named for its scimitar (saber)-shaped horns, lives on the edges of the Sahara desert.

The lakes and rivers of Africa provide life-giving water and are a major means of transportation from one place to another. They are also the habitat of an important source of protein—fish—to millions of Africans, as well as the habitat of some ferocious beasts.

The River Horse and the Pebble Worm

One of the strangest animals to be found bobbing around in an African lake or river is the hippopotamus. Its name means "river horse" in Greek, but it's nothing like a horse. For one thing, adult males can weigh as much as a pickup truck.

Hippos don't eat in the water. They merely use water as a daytime refuge from the sun and from predators like lions and hyenas, which target young hippos particularly. After a day of bobbing about in the water, keeping cool and socializing, the hippos leave the lakes and rivers at dusk and wander along well-worn trails up to 10 miles inland to graze.

Despite its monstrous mouth and huge teeth, the hippo eats only grass. It moves along like a giant lawn mower, clipping the grass as short as golf course grass with its lips. A hippo uses the big teeth to defend itself and intimidate other hippos.

Here's some good advice: never get between a hippo and the lake or river in which it lives. To get back to the safety of the water, it will run right over whatever is in its way like a freight train. Hippos don't

like to be disturbed in the water either and will bite a small fishing boat in half. In fact, every year, hippos kill more people than any other African animal, including snakes and lions (but not including the malaria parasite).

Crocodiles, which used to be called "pebble worms" by the ancient Romans, are just about everywhere in African rivers and many lakes. They lived during the age of the dinosaurs and are one of the oldest large animals on earth. They are also the largest reptiles. A big one can be almost 20 feet long and easily eat a small human in a couple of chomps.

The crocodile's traplike jaws are designed only to open and shut, and the teeth are designed to grip rather than bite or chew. The toothed trap snaps over a whole fish, or over an exposed part of a large prey item such as the leg of a bird or an antelope.

Hippos in shallow water.

Crocodile sunning on a riverbank.

Once it bites, the crocodile moves in reverse, pulling its prey into the water and then spinning its whole body around with a corkscrew snap of its massive tail. Chunks of meat and bone are twisted off like pieces of toffee and swallowed whole.

Grasslands, Woodlands, and Bushlands

Most of Africa is grassland. A grassland is a habitat in which the main vegetation is—guess what?—grass. Rolling grasslands dotted with flat-topped acacia trees are part of the picture of Africa familiar to most North Americans.

Woodlands or wooded grasslands are grasslands with lots of trees, but with fewer trees than forests and with trees that are not as tall as trees in forests.

African wooded grassland.

Woodland tree canopies are said to be open; that is, the leaves of one tree generally don't touch those of the neighboring trees.

Bushlands or bushed grasslands are grasslands with more shrubs than trees. Grasslands that have a mixture of trees and shrubs are called, not too surprisingly, bushed and wooded grasslands. Grasslands are also called savannas. Got it?

African grasslands are home to many of the largest mammals in the world. These habitats are so vast that a walk from the Sahara Desert to Cape Town in the far south, more than 4,000 miles, would mainly cross through various types of grassland.

The number of trees growing in the grasslands depends on local soil types and the amount of rainfall that area receives. It also depends on how animals and humans have affected the ecosystem. Animals, particularly big ones like elephants and giraffes, eat trees and shrubs and keep them from becoming too numerous. People chop down trees and light grass fires that burn off shrubs and sometimes kill young trees.

Fine Woods

At the far southern tip of Africa a vegetation type grows that is so special it has been called one of the wonders of the world. It's known as *fynbos* (FEYN-boss), which means "fine woods" in Afrikaans. *Fynbos* only covers about 35,000 square miles, about the size of Indiana, but it contains 8,600 species of plants, of which 5,800 are native to the region.

Fynbos might look like boring, bushy scrubland, with lots of low, twisted woody plants and only a few trees here and there. But when it rains, millions of plants blossom, and the area looks like the biggest flower garden in the world. The national flower of the Republic of South Africa is the protea (pro-TE-yah). It only grows in the South African *fynbos*.

The Big Five

All over the African grasslands, where there are few human settlements around, magnificent animals are still roaming free, like the so-called Big Five: elephant, rhinoceros, buffalo, lion, and leopard.

In bygone days, the Big Five were the favorite targets of big game hunters, mainly white colonials, who spent weeks in the bush on a safari, looking for animals to kill. They didn't travel light. Each safari needed 100 "native" porters to carry the white men's tents and beds, tables and chairs, pots and pans, food and water, gin and tonics, sometimes even a record player, and, of course, guns and ammunition.

The hunters were usually guided by tough, lean Africans who knew how to track wild animals and pick up on the signs the animals left behind. They would help the hunters stalk a lion or buffalo for hours, position the hunters downwind, and move in as close as possible. The hunter might pause to admire the beauty and grandeur of the animal and then shoot it with a powerful rifle.

After the hunters posed for a nice picture of themselves with the dead animal, the African gun bearers' assistants skinned the beast, cut off its head, salted down the wet bits, put the trophy in a sack, and carried it for a week back to a taxidermist in Nairobi, Johannesburg, Leopoldville, or Dakar, depending on where the safari was in Africa.

Skins would end up on the floor of the hunter's study, the mounted head would snarl or snort out of

Lion.

the walls. An elephant's tusks would be carved into chess pieces or bangles; the elephant's feet made into umbrella stands. Disgusting? You bet!

The lion, often called the "king of beasts," is really kind of lazy. A pride of lions will sleep for hours at a time. Like most carnivores, they can afford long rest periods between high-protein meals. The females do most of the work chasing and killing big prey like buffalo, wildebeests, and zebras. The females cooperate with each other in the hunt, with one lioness lying in wait while the others chase the prey into the ambush. Just as the lionesses are about to enjoy their catch, a couple of big male lions will come and chase them away and eat the choice bits.

Leopards are sleek, solitary, and stealthy nocturnal hunters who kill and eat antelopes, which are somewhat smaller than typical lion prey. They are so strong that they can carry a 120-pound impala clamped in their jaws as they climb straight up an acacia tree trunk. Leopards often have to hide their kills in trees to keep the meat safe for a couple of days from lions and hyenas. Their secretive lifestyle allows them to live undisturbed close to villages, from which they can steal an occasional goat.

Buffalo are the meanest, ugliest beasts in the grasslands. Some people consider them more dangerous than hippos, maybe because it is more likely that you would bump into one when walking in the bush. Buffalo wounded by hunters have been known to track down the hunters with murderous intent. Maybe that's only fair. They live in large mixed herds, including males, females, and their young. After sitting around chewing cud like a bunch of cattle, the buffalo vote on which way to go next. They stand up one by one, and the direction in which most are pointing is the way they will wander off.

African Cape buffalo.

Leopard.

Rhinoceroses are prehistoric, ponderous beasts who usually live alone except during mating time or when a mother is nursing her calf. There are two species. The black rhino is a browser that eats mainly wildflowers and the tender leaf shoots on bushes with its flexible, prehensile upper lip. The so-called white rhino, from southern Africa, is exclusively a grazer. It mows grass with its wide lips. In fact, the white rhino isn't white at all. Its name comes from the Afrikaans word for wide, which is *wit*. The rhino's famous horns are actually fused and hardened hair and are used by males fighting over females and by females protecting their young from hyenas and lions.

Black rhinoceros mother and calf.

Elephants. Everything about them is big. The world's largest land mammal, adult bulls can stand 12 feet at their shoulders and weigh 10,000 pounds. Elephants have the biggest teeth of any animal. The largest tusk ever recorded was on an elephant from Benin; it weighed 258 pounds. By the way, tusks are not canine or eye teeth, but highly modified incisors—biting teeth. Elephant molars are huge as well, 10 inches long. Elephants have the longest pregnancies—22 months, nearly two years—of any animal. They have long life spans, second only to humans, and long childhoods. Like human kids, a young male elephant stays with his family group until puberty, around 14 years of age. A female calf may stay with her mother and sisters for the rest of her life.

Elephants are big hearted, too. There are many recorded instances of elephants helping one another—supporting and trying to lift an injured comrade, pulling a spear from another's backside, pulling youngsters out of mud holes, and females helping other females give birth, just like human midwives.

Elephant society is matriarchal, meaning the females call the shots. The oldest adult female, the matriarch, leads the family group. Because elephants live so long and wander over such a large area, it is vital for the survival of the group that someone remembers all the good places to go for food and water, as well as all the bad places to avoid because of danger or drought.

When young bulls leave their families, they hang around with groups of other males but only become big and strong enough to compete for females about 20 years later. That's a long time to wait for a girlfriend.

My Horn Is My Dilemma

The horn nearly caused the rhino's extinction. Because there is a demand for rhino horn outside of Africa, poachers have hunted both black and white rhinos to the brink of extinction. Can you imagine what could be so valuable that humans must have it, even at the expense of an entire species? Yemeni men use the rhino horn as decoration. They wear ceremonial daggers in belts called *jembiyas* (jem-BEE-yah) that have handles made from rhino horn. In China and other east Asian countries, horns are ground into powder and used in medicines thought to make men more virile. What will people do when there are no more rhinos?

Write an African Fable

Africans are fond of telling fantastic stories to their kids and to each other. Sometimes the stories simply relate some exciting or important event that happened yesterday or sometime in the past, but usually they are fanciful fables.

Fables are folk stories that often feature animal characters who behave and speak as human beings. The story is often meant to illustrate human silliness and weaknesses. It might also try to explain the origin of something, like the San Bushmen story on page 35 that tells why the hippo scatters its dung. A fable usually teaches a lesson or suggests a better way of doing things. A moral, which is a short recipe for better behavior, often conveys the purpose of the fable and is sometimes directly stated at the end. Remember Aesop's fable of the tortoise and the hare? The moral was "slow and steady wins the race."

Here's a typical fable told by the Shona people of South Africa:

One day Elephant met Squirrel on the path to the river. Proud and lordly, Elephant swept Squirrel off the path with his trunk and rumbled, "Out of my way, you of small size and even less importance."

Squirrel was greatly offended. He stamped his little feet in a rage and decided he would teach Elephant some manners.

"Hey!" shouted Squirrel indignantly. "You may be very large, and you may be very proud, and I know you think you're the greatest animal on earth, but you are much mistaken!"

Elephant looked 'round in surprise. "I am not mistaken, lowly Squirrel," he rumbled. "I am the greatest, and all animals know that."

"Let me tell you something, o Elephant," chattered Squirrel angrily, flicking his tail. "I may be small, but I can eat 10 times as much as you! I challenge you to an eating contest. I wager that I, Squirrel, will eat more palm nuts and eat for a longer time than you, high and mighty elephant!"

Elephant trumpeted with laughter. He was so amused that he accepted Squirrel's ridiculous challenge. Besides, he was rather fond of palm nuts. So both animals collected a huge pile of palm nuts, divided it into two equal piles, and agreed to start the contest the next morning. Elephant could hardly wait. He even skipped his evening meal of acacia seedpods so as to be very hungry the morning. He intended to put Squirrel firmly in his place.

At dawn the next day the two contestants started to eat.

Elephant munched steadily through his pile. Squirrel nibbled away furiously and was soon full. When he saw Elephant reaching for another nut with his trunk tip, Squirrel quietly slipped away and sent a cousin who was hiding nearby to take his place. Throughout the morning, brothers, sisters, cousins, uncles, aunts—one hungry squirrel after another—slipped in to take a turn at the nut pile. Elephant was so absorbed in his own eating that he didn't notice.

At midday, Elephant looked up. "Well, Squirrel, have you had your fill yet?" He was surprised to see that not only was his little adversary still eating, but his pile of palm nuts was disappearing almost as fast as Elephant's own.

"Not yet!" mumbled Squirrel with his mouth full. "And you?"

"Of course not!" came the gruff reply. And Elephant started to eat faster.

By the time the sun was setting, Elephant was so full he could hardly stand. He looked over to where Squirrel (the original one, who had come back after a day of sleeping in a nearby tree) was still eating more palm nuts. Elephant groaned a long, low rumble.

"Truly, you are amazing, Squirrel," he said. "I cannot go on, and I'm forced to admit that you have won the contest." He lifted his trunk and trumpeted a salute.

Squirrel, hopping with delight, thanked Elephant and told him not to be so proud in the future. And from that day to this one, Elephant has always shown great respect for Squirrel.

The moral of that story might be "Pride goeth before destruction, and a haughty spirit before a fall."

Try your hand at writing an African fable.

You'll need

The list of characteristics that Africans from many different ethnic groups attribute to various animals, found on page 47.
Pencil
Paper

1. Use the list on page 47 to choose your characters and their corresponding qualities. Characters in the fable can also be human or even otherworldly. Sometimes God is a character, as in the San Bushmen's hippo tale.

2. See if you can think of a moral for your fable that would be instructive, say, for your little sister who gets into your things or the older kid who gives you nasty looks.

3. Start writing. Keep the style simple, with short sentences, as though you were telling the story around a campfire. The fable shouldn't be too complicated or too long; a couple of pages should do. Did you note in the sample fable that typically the article "the" is dropped in front of the animal's name? The animal name becomes a proper noun.

4. Ask a couple of friends to read your fable.

There are two species of African elephants, the common savanna elephant and the smaller, secretive forest elephant that lives deep in the heart of the Congo rainforest.

Elephants are intelligent by any animal standard, like chimps. They appear to be aware of themselves as individuals in a group. They have long memories about places and other animals, human or elephant. They use primitive tools, like a stick held in the trunk to scratch themselves or a log moved under a tree to stand on and reach a tasty fruit. They even have a language of nearly 100 very low-frequency sounds that sound like tummy rumbles but really function as words with individual meanings. In summary, along with apes and cetaceans (set-TAY-shuns), the animal group that includes whales, dolphins, and porpoises, elephants are among the most intelligent animals on earth.

How do you measure intelligence? This young female is using a tool. She picked up a stick of just the right size and used it to scratch her chest.

Wandering Wildebeest

What's the greatest show on earth? The annual wildebeest migration between the Serengeti National Park in Tanzania and the Maasai Mara Game Reserve in Kenya. Every year, nearly two million migrating grazers—wildebeest, zebra, Thomson's gazelle, and

eland—travel in a 300-mile circle in search of green grass. As they travel, they stomp through the home ranges of some 300,000 other herbivores, resident animals like topi, buffalo, giraffe, hartebeeste, Grant's gazelle, waterbuck, and warthog. Along the way, the wildebeest are in constant danger from lurking predators—lions, hyenas, leopards, cheetahs, hunting dogs, and jackals. Vultures soar above waiting for a kill, and dung beetles scurry around below collecting droppings to lay their eggs in.

These aren't ants. They're some of the million wildebeests that migrate each year from Tanzania's Serengeti National Park to the Maasai Mara Game Reserve in Kenya and back again.

Wildebeest or white-bearded gnu (it's pretty obvious how the gnu earned the nickname "white-bearded"), with zebra in the African dust.

The star of the show is the foolish wildebeest, also called a white-bearded gnu (guh-NEW). Smaller than a buffalo, bigger than a gazelle, the gnu is about the size of a Maasai cow. It looks goofy, and the way it leaps about during the mating season makes it the mad cow of the Serengeti grasslands.

Africa used to have many migrations like that of the Serengeti. For example, the tiang migration in southern Sudan, the blue wildebeests in southern Africa, and elephants just about everywhere. But, today, the ancient migration routes have been mostly cut off by a growing human population and an increasing number of settlements and farms.

After the Big Five, the Small-to-Medium Zillion

The Big Five and even the Serengeti wildebeests are just a drop in the bucket compared to the many different kinds of animals in Africa. There are nearly 1,200 other mammal species in Africa, from aardvarks to zorillas.

Lions and leopards aren't the only predators in Africa. Africa is home to cheetahs; three species of hyenas; wild dogs; Abyssinian wolves; honey badgers; weasels (four species); skunk equivalents—zorillas; jackals (three species); foxes (seven species); cats (seven species, not including the big ones); 14 species of genets and civets; 30 species of insect

The pyramid of life in Africa. Spot the carnivores and herbivores and decomposers.

eaters like shrews, moles, and hedgehogs; more bats than you can shake a stick at; and termite eaters like the four species of pangolins and aardvarks.

Wildebeests may put on a spectacular show, but don't forget all the other herbivores that live in Africa. There are zebras (four species including the wild ass); hippos; six species of pigs; giraffes; okapis; various large, spiral-horned animals (including bushbucks, bongos, and elands); nine different dwarf antelopes; four dik-diks; three kobs; five reed-bucks; a dozen species of gazelles; seven long-faced antelopes (including wildebeest, topi, and harte-beeste); six so-called horselike antelopes (such as roan, sable, and oryx); Barbary sheep; Nubian ibex;

one deer (in North Africa); a kind of deer-pig called a water chevrotain (CHEV-row-tainh); and—the elephant's cousin—three species of hyrax. Is that all? No way. Africa is also teeming with hares, rabbits, squirrels, porcupines, spring hares, gundis, cane rats, gerbils, dormice, mole rats, and mice.

Then, of course, there are the great apes (three species), the baboons (eight species), 57 varieties of monkey, 20 different bush babies, and three pottos.

And that doesn't even touch on the 2,000 species of birds, 1,800 species of freshwater fish, varieties of marine mammals like whales and dol-phins, thousands of butterflies, and countless bee-tles. And plants? Don't even start . . .

Animal Fetishes

Most ancient African statues are shaped like animals and are intended to be used as fetishes (FEH-tish), or charms believed to contain magical powers.

Bakongo witch doctors or spiritual healers in central Africa make animal fetishes called *nkisi* (nn-KEY-see). The pieces of metal hammered into the *nkisi*'s wooden body serve as antennae to ward off evil spirits and any bad wishes of mischievous neighbors.

A special *nkisi* with two heads is called an *nkondi* (nn-CON-dee). The one pictured here, from the Kongo tribe in the Democratic Republic of the Congo, has two doglike heads with sharp teeth. With their red eyes they watch for danger from each direction and stare down would-be thieves. Pieces of human bone are wedged between the bristles to suggest what happened to previous intruders. *Nkondi* were also believed to be effective in witnessing public events. Each time an agreement was made, an oath taken, or a punishment declared, a nail or piece of metal was driven into the *nkondi* to seal the deal. The participants would then know that the *nkondi* was watching carefully to make certain that no promises would be broken, or else.

Usually an *nkondi* has a hole somewhere in its body where special items are inserted, such as hair, bones, pieces of precious stone, medicines, or money.

Nkondi nkisi: a watchdog fetish from the Congo.

Animal Meanings

Being surrounded by such a diversity of animals may explain why Africans have traditionally been great naturalists, living in harmony with most animals. Africans attribute different characteristics to different animals and use the animals as characters in stories or symbols in religion. Here is a gallery of African animals and their special meanings to different African peoples.

Aardvark: ridiculous, ambiguous, and sly. The ancient Egyptians used the aardvark to represent Set, the god of chaos and confusion. Set was believed to devour the moon each month to keep the night dark.

African hare: small, but cunning and resourceful. The Dogon people in Mali use a hare mask in dances in which the hare tricks large animals like lions and elephants.

Bats: spirits of the dead and allies of sorcerers.

Buffalo: powerful and enduring. The Dan of eastern Liberia use a buffalo mask to summon power to drive out evil.

Chameleon: wise and cautious. A chameleon adorns a wooden dance prop used by the Afo people in Nigeria.

Elephant: powerful and orderly. The elephant handle on a Zimbabwean box is used to keep valuables safe.

Make an Nkondi Nkisi

You can make your own *nkondi* from wood and other materials found around your home.

Make an *nkondi* and keep it in your room to protect and aid you and to ward off evil spirits or annoying brothers or sisters. You can pound a nail into your *nkondi* each time you want to celebrate an achievement or make a promise.

Adult supervision required

You'll need

Hammer

36 #4 panel nails

2 2-inch by 4-inch by 12-inch pieces of softwood

Small can of red paint

Paintbrush

4 1-inch by 2-inch by 4-inch pieces of softwood

Glue

4–6 common 4-inch nails

4–8 carpet tacks

4 red bottle caps

Black marker or 1 small can of black paint

Plasticine (a plastic "clay" used for making models)

A number of nails and screws of any size and condition

Screwdriver

1. Hammer eight evenly spaced panel nails into the ends of each of the 2-inch by 4-inch by 12-inch pieces of wood to form the teeth of the *nkondi*. One-quarter inch of each nail should be left protruding from the wood.

2. On both of the 2-inch by 4-inch by 12-inch pieces, paint the inside of the mouth between the teeth red. Let dry.

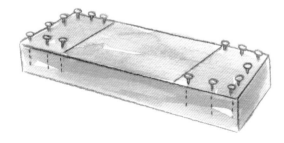

3. Glue the 1-inch by 2-inch by 4-inch wood strips to both sides of one of the 2-inch by 4-inch by 12-inch pieces about three inches from the ends or just inside the teeth.

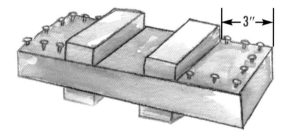

4. Hammer two of the 2-inch by 4-inch by 12-inch pieces together using the 4-inch common nails (make sure that the *nkondi*'s teeth are pointing inward).

5. Use the carpet tacks to attach the bottle caps to the sides of the *nkondi* as "eyes." You may want to add a line of black with paint or a marker to make it look more ferocious. You

could also add a couple of carpet tacks to both front ends as nostrils.

6. Put some objects into the holes in the *nkondi*'s side. Common things would include locks of hair or small photos of your family or friends (so the *nkondi* knows who to protect), special things you want it to keep safe, a penny for good luck, and so on). Seal the holes with a blob of plasticine.

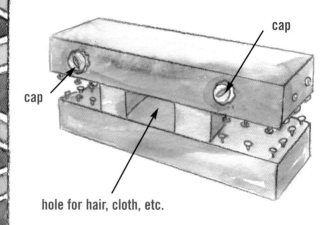

cap

cap

hole for hair, cloth, etc.

7. Finally, hammer old nails and add screws into the *nkondi*'s back and side as shown in the photo. Leave room for extra nails.

Your *nkondi nkisi* is now finished until you need to drive a new nail into it to make a deal with yourself or others. Display it in a prominent place in your room or house, so it can watch over you.

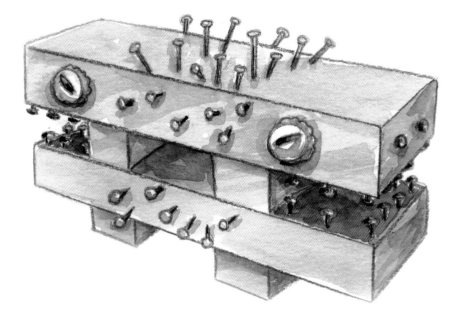

Frogs: resurrection from the dead.

Hippopotamus: godmother. In Mozambique it is believed that hippos are goddesses that rule over a wonderful green land under the water.

Honey badger: fearless against all odds. The *nkisi* watchdog from Congo looks like a honey badger who will bite any intruders to the home.

Hyena: foolish; often the ally of sorcerers and witches. This Bamana hyena dance mask is from Mali.

Leopard: bold and cunning. The leopard was represented on the currency notes in the Democratic Republic of Congo when the dictator Mobutu Sese-Seko was in power. Below is a leopard made form bronze.

Lion: regal, charming, strong, and loyal. The lion is the symbol of the king or chief in many African tribes. Often a god takes on the form of a lion when revealing the god's presence to humans.

Owl: omen of death. Verreaux's eagle-owl is one of the largest owls in the world. This menacing owl sculpture was made by Kenya's "junkyard" artist Kioko, who makes animals out of scrap metal.

Porcupine: defensive power. Although porcupines are a major pest to farmers' crops, the Akan-speaking people of Ghana use their images to defend against invasion from enemies.

Snake: teacher of the art of healing. Often more respected than feared, snake fetishes and charms are used to heal and protect. This snake carving is from Cameroon.

Tortoise: intelligent and prudent. All tribes treat old man tortoise with respect.

Make a Snake Bracelet

In this activity, you'll make a snake bracelet or armband for yourself or for a friend by braiding four strands of thick copper wire.

Why so many people are scared of snakes is not easy to understand. Hippos, reckless taxi drivers, and armed conflicts kill far more people in Africa each year than snakes do. Nevertheless, the rock python (Africa's largest snake) and the Gabon viper (one of the most poisonous species are the snakes most frequently represented in ominous-looking carvings and statues. Even a simple bracelet made from copper wire can represent a snake. The snake is your friend since it is on your wrist. But what it might do to your enemies we can only guess.

Adult supervision required

You'll need

1 yard of thick, single-strand copper wire
Wire cutters
A nail in a fence plank or other wooden surface
Quick-dry epoxy glue
2 red beeds

1. Cut the wire into two equal halves using the wire cutters. You should then have two pieces, each about 18 inches long.
2. Bend both wires in half and hang them over the nail.
3. Separate the wire into four strands, two in each hand. Make a mental note of their numbers, one through four, left to right. The braid you will use repeats this pattern.
4. The far outside right-hand strand (#4 in diagram A) goes under the middle two (#2 and #3), up over #2, and back to the right to take up the position that #3 was in originally.
5. Then, the far left strand (#1 in diagram B) goes to the right, underneath the middle two (now #2 and #4), up over #4, and back to the left.

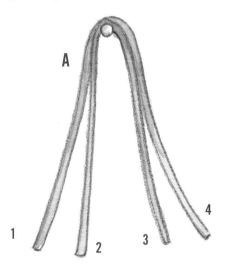

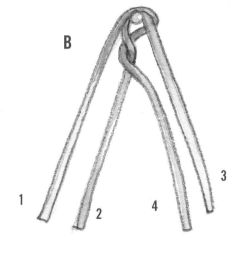

6. Repeat steps 4 and 5, starting now with #3 on the outside right, as in diagram C, then next with #2 in diagram D on the outside left, then #4 on the outside right in diagram E, and so on until the wire is finished (diagram F).

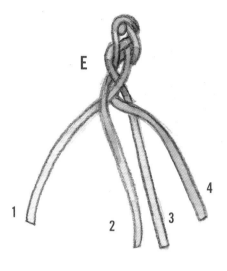

E

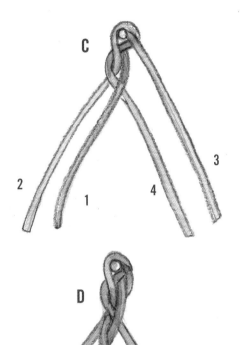

C

D

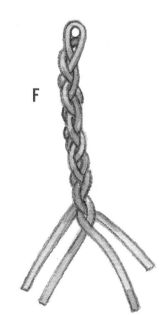

F

7. Remove the braid from the nail, twist the ends together, bend the braid around your wrist to check the size (leave about ¼–½ inch between the ends), and cut the loose end to size. Straighten it out again.

8. In order to round the cut ends of the wire, dip the loose end of the bracelet into a small blob of quick-dry epoxy glue, turning the end to transfer as much of the glue as possible to it. Let dry and repeat several times if necessary until a suitable snake head is built up.

9. On the last layer, add two red beads at a spacing that makes them look like snake eyes.

10. Let dry. Then bend the bracelet back into shape and put it on or give it to a friend to ward off evil spirits.

Animal Behavior: Feeding, Fleeing, Feeling Good, and Finding a Mate

The African landscape is alive with activity. In fact, animals are always doing something, even when they are asleep. And everything they do is useful to them, even playing.

Scientists are fond of classifying. They make long lists of organisms or objects and then sort them into groups or categories. It is possible to group animals' daily activities into just four categories, the four *F*s: feeding, fleeing, feeling good, and finding a mate. If you can find an animal not behaving in one of those ways, you could write the first book about it.

Feeding

Feeding involves far more than biting, chewing, and swallowing. Those are important parts of the feeding process, but there are several actions to be accomplished first. For example, an animal has to find the food, which usually takes some work because most food would rather not be found.

Finding food is easy for herbivores because plants are usually abundant, and they never run away. Carnivores have to work much harder for a meal. A lioness, for example, first has to identify a potential victim. When there are more than a million wildebeests wandering over the Serengeti Plains, she could spend a lot of time deciding which one to go for. She might select the one limping on a sore leg; it probably cannot run very fast.

Next the lioness stalks slowly and carefully through long grass so the target is not spooked too early.

Lioness stalking.

A short frantic chase, a pounce, and a wrestling match follow as the 300-pound cat tries to hold down and kill a wildebeest that may be even heavier than she is. Finally, the female lion, who has done all the work, has to chase away marauding male lions or troublesome hyenas. But the high-protein meal is worth the effort.

Fleeing

Fleeing is the most conspicuous action an animal can make to avoid a predator. However, if the prey cannot be seen, the predator cannot catch it. This is

The Best Defense Is a Good Offense

The physical characteristics of some animals assist them in both getting food and defending themselves. The three-horned chameleon preys on insects. It is also vulnerable to an attack from birds of prey. It has developed skin that changes color to match the background. The near-perfect camouflage allows it to sneak up on insects while at the same time escaping notice by hawks.

Chameleon.

Poisonous snakes like the puff adder use their venom to subdue large prey as well as to defend themselves against attack.

Mouths to Match the Meal

Different species of herbivores have evolved in many different ways, developing body parts to get at and eat plants, from the ground to the treetops.

Hippopotamuses' lips are a foot wide to mow short grass.

Hippo.

Giraffes' necks are extra long to so they can nibble nutritious acacia tree leaves. Their leathery tongues are 18 inches long and covered with especially gooey saliva to cope with the acacia's fierce thorns.

Giraffes.

Elephants' trunks can reach as high as giraffes stand to reach tree leaves or as low as the hippos stoop to harvest great bundles of grass.

Elephant feeding.

The African buffalo has wide lips like a cow's for efficient grazing, whereas its cousin the Grant's gazelle has a narrow mouth, more like a goat, for selecting certain herbs that grow among the grass.

Grant's gazelle.

Most insects are herbivores as well. Weevil beetles have pointed mouth parts to pierce leaves so they can suck out the juices. Leaf-cutting ants use their pinchers like garden shears.

Ant.

Weevil.

Slugs and snails have raspy tongues to scrape off the top layer of green leaves.

Slug.

why many herbivores have camouflage coloration and use behaviors like keeping alert and staying very still when predators are nearby.

As a last resort, a cornered animal will turn and put up a fight, even if the outcome seems hopeless. A lucky lunge with the horns might just stop the predator's attack. The oryx (see page 35) cannot run very fast because it lives in hot, arid areas. But it has long, sharp horns and is one of the few herbivores known to have killed a lion by spearing it.

Feeling Good

Feeling good and being comfortable is not just about loafing. It's really a description of spare time behavior that animals (and people) exhibit when they are not busy with getting food, fleeing, or finding a mate. These activities include scratching, washing, bathing in dust, preening, resting, and playing.

Elephant calf playing with his older sister.

Comfort behaviors are important because they keep the body clean and parasite-free and the animal rested, ready for anything. Playing is not frivolous because it provides animals with opportunities to exercise their muscles, learn about peers, and practice hunting moves.

Finding a Mate

Finding a mate and reproducing is as complicated a business for animals as it is for humans. There are several stages: courtship, mating, giving birth, and raising the young.

During courtship, males display their virility to females in often complicated rituals. These rituals show the females that the males are fit and strong, free from parasites, and full of good health and energy. During the courting period, a male suitor will have to fight off other males. He will also need to be strong enough to defend the female and young in the future. All of the attention the males pay to her stimulates the female's hormone system to begin producing eggs and get ready for mating.

The main challenge male animals encounter during mating is getting the female to hold still long enough that the male can begin the reproduction process. The bull elephant lays his trunk along the female's back to stop her running off. Her decision to stay suggests that she wants to mate with the male. The male leopard tortoise makes a peculiar barking noise. The female seems to stop and listen. The male lion rather roughly bites the female's neck.

Males Showing Off

Males spend much energy, display bright colors, and even grow special body features (like big horns, long tails, and head crests) to attract potential mates.

A weaverbird displays at a nest.

This male masked weaver has built a lovely nest and flaps his wings and sings like crazy while a prospective female inspects the premises.

Wildebeests fighting.

Why the Zebra Got Its Stripes

"'That's curious,' said the Leopard. 'I suppose it is because we have just come in out of the sunshine. I can smell Zebra, and I can hear Zebra, but I can't see Zebra.'"

—Rudyard Kipling,
"How the Leopard Got Its Spots"

No one is quite sure why one of Africa's most eye-catching animals is colored the way it is. Scientists cannot agree. Some say the wider stripes on the

Grevy's zebra: narrow stripes.

Burchell's zebra's rump may confuse the charging lioness and cause her to miss her prey when she pounces. Others say that from a distance, the stripes help camouflage the shape of the Grevy's zebra. Still others argue that the stripes have evolved to help keep the zebra family group together, since zebras are attracted to striped objects and tend to follow them.

What do you think?

Burchell's zebra: broad stripes.

Mating in animals is usually over in the blink of an eye, except with rhinos. There mating may take as long as a half hour.

The time of the year when the young are developing, either in the mother's womb or as eggs in a nest, is the riskiest time for the female. This is why most females are camouflage colored. The female ostrich sits on the nest of two dozen eggs during the day. Her dull brown plumage blends perfectly with the dry-season grass. The black-and-white male takes his turn sitting on the nest at night.

Defending young animals from attack and getting them enough food to grow strong are exhausting tasks for parents. No animals on earth are as fearless as a mother defending her young. A female wildebeest will put herself between her calf and a hyena when he is chasing them both. A tiny sunbird will dive-bomb a monitor lizard 100 times her size to distract him from the nest. A sitting ostrich will intimidate an approaching rhino.

Finding a mate and raising a family are really what all the other behaviors are about. Feeding, fleeing, and feeling good behaviors are designed to keep animals alive and fit. Why? So they live long enough to produce offspring. Those young animals will have many of the advantageous characteristics that allowed the parents to reach maturity. This means that the offspring have a good chance of surviving long enough to have young of their own. And so it goes, from generation to generation.

Become a Field Biologist

**Field guides to various species of animals are helpful tools for any field biologist.
Use them to deepen your study of your chosen animals.**

In this activity you will use the same careful observation techniques that scientists use in the African bush to compare the daily behavior of different species of animals. For example, compare your cat or dog (carnivores) with a cow or a parakeet (herbivores). You might choose a friend or family member to serve as an example of an omnivore. If you live close to a zoo, you should have lots of choices, although the behaviors might not be very natural, particularly since feeding time is decided by the zookeepers, not the animals.

You'll need

Pencil

Pad of paper

Binoculars

Wristwatch

Tape recorder (optional)

Field guides to birds, mammals, etc. (optional)

1. Gather your equipment and decide what species you will study. If you choose a human, make certain that you get his or her permission to be your subject.

2. Study each species during the same time period over two consecutive days. Use your binoculars if the animal is small or far away. Try to choose two days with roughly the same weather forecast; this will help make the results more comparable.

3. Make a table with headings across the top that list the four main behavior systems: FEEDING, FLEEING, FEELING GOOD, and FINDING A MATE. There should be spaces for marking down your observations and a column along the left to indicate the time intervals. You could use one-hour, half-hour, or 15-minute periods if you decide to sample during a limited time period.

Behavior Observation Datasheet

Species Observed: *neighbor's cat (tabby)*

Location: *neighbor's backyard*

Researcher: (your name here)

Methodology: *interval sampling, every 5 minutes*

Date: (date here)

Weather: *cool (52 deg.), overcast, light breeze from SW*

Time	Feeding	Fleeing	Feeling Good	Finding a Mate	Comments
	searching, attacking, chasing, killing, eating, excreting	hiding, freezing, running away	scratching, washing, preening, resting, sleeping, playing	courting, mating, fighting, nest-building, caring for young	
6:00–7:00 A.M.	IIII		IIII III		drank milk from bowl, fell asleep on porch
7:00–8:00 A.M.		II	IIII IIII		chased up tree by dog, slept on branch
8:00–9:00 A.M.	III		IIII IIII		stalked bird in tree—missed bird, came down, licked fur, slept
9:00–10:00 A.M.			IIII IIII I	I	sleeping most of time, chased our cat out of yard
10:00–11:00 A.M.			IIII IIII II		sleeping, scratched couple of times
11:00 A.M.–12:00 P.M.	III		IIII IIII		neighbor put out cat food, sits watching birds for 10 min, back to sleep
Total	10	2	59	I	

4. Use two observation techniques used by researchers who study animals like baboons and elephants. One is called "focal animal sampling" and the other is "interval sampling."

In focal sampling you observe everything that your animal does and put a mark in the correct column during the particular time interval. (Many field biologists use a tape recorder and dictate their observations onto it, especially if their animals are fast-moving primates or predators.) However, some animals will exhibit some behaviors over longer periods of time, like a cow grazing or your cat sleeping. The trick here is to use "interval sampling" and put a mark in the column for FEELING GOOD for the sleeping cat over fixed time intervals, for example, every five minutes. If your cat sleeps for half an hour, between 8:12 and 8:42, your data sheet would have 14 or 15 tick marks under FEELING GOOD in the period from 8:00 to 9:00 A.M.

As you sit waiting for your cat to do something, you will realize that the work of the field biologist is not always filled with exciting elephant chases. You may want to take a book along to pass the time.

When the cat wakes up, it might stretch (put a tick under FEELING GOOD for the stretch), then start stalking a bird. You would immediately put a tick under FEEDING. If it stalks the bird for more than 10 minutes, you might add another tick under FEEDING.

You may want to record more detailed information by working out a code for each type of behavior. For example, you could use a *sl* for sleeping to distinguish it from *st* for stretching.

At the end of the day or half day, you will have a data sheet full of tick marks or letter codes. It is now time for data analysis.

5. Add up the marks in each column and make a bar chart. This graph will display a comparison of how much time the animal spent doing each kind of behavior.

If you have studied an herbivore and a carnivore, you can compare their charts. What differences would you expect to see between them? Herbivores have to spend much more time eating to get enough protein and energy to survive. Carnivore meals tend to be highly nutritious, so carnivores can afford to spend more time sleeping. Does your data show this?

You can also analyze which behaviors occur at different times of day by counting the events in the early rows, say 6–9, and comparing them to the latter rows, 10–12. If you have chosen a bird, like the carnivorous hawk or seed-eating cardinal, you will probably see much more activity in the earlier hours. You can make a chart to show these kinds of differences. Can you think of any more kinds of comparisons you can make based on your data?

Part Three

African People and Places

The Family of Humans

Genes are little chunks of information that work like tiny computer programs in our body cells. They help determine what we look like and how we behave. Geneticists are scientists who study genes, DNA, and the ways parents pass on their genes and characteristics to their kids from generation to generation.

Geneticists have cracked many of the secret code of our genes. They have found that every human being on earth carries some genes from just one African woman who lived about 140,000 years ago—some 6,000 human generations in the past. She is the original African "Eve," great-great-great-great- (and so on) grandmother of us all. Geneticists have found that the ancient African who is great-great-great-great- (and so on) grandfather to us all lived only about 60,000 years ago. He must have had children with one of African Eve's great-great-great- (and so on) grandkids, so that makes him a kind of African "Adam."

So if there ever was a "Garden of Eden," it would have been in Africa.

Exodus

Scientists now believe that modern humans started migrating from Africa to Asia, Europe, and beyond about 80,000 years ago. This is how it might have happened. An early *Homo erectus* family in Ngorongoro Crater near Olduvai (OLD-due-vie)

First Tool

Our early ancestors used rocks to break open nuts, kill animals, or attack each other during fights. Some started to notice that a rock with a sharp edge was better for cutting and killing.

One bright fellow, maybe when he lost his favorite rock or more likely when his mate suggested the improvement to him, thought to himself, "If only I could make a sharp edge on any rock, I would always have a handy *mffzzggg*" (they didn't have a word for "ax" yet).

A hand ax in a workshop in northern Kenya.

He tried a few different rocks and banged around a bit until he discovered that a certain kind of flinty stone worked best. If you hit it with another stone just so, a flake would break off and leave a very sharp edge. Not only that, his mate noticed that the flake, if it was big enough, could work well as a *vzzggmm* (they didn't have a word for "knife" yet).

It wasn't long before the original bashing rock became a hand ax. And the news spread like wildfire.

Pretty soon everyone was making hand axes, or so it seems, since some archaeological sites in Africa have piles of them. One of the most famous sites where hand axes have been found is in Olduvai Gorge in Tanzania, which is also where Louis and Mary Leakey discovered the oldest human remains, including that of *Homo habilis*, nicknamed "Handyman." "Handyperson" would have been a more appropriate name, since women were inventing tools too.

Create Rock Art

Wear old clothes during this activity so you don't have to worry about getting paint on them.

Africans were the first artists on earth. They painted pictures of animals on the sides of rocks and the insides of caves. Cave paintings and rock carvings have been found throughout Africa. So what is cave art for? Think of some of the uses for drawing and painting today, such as recording history (a painting of a historic battle or famous person), teaching (a sketch in a cookbook), recording ordinary life (holiday snapshots), praising a great leader or deity (painted icons in a church), or decorating and expressing emotion (modern art or graffiti in the subway). In fact, cave paintings were used to serve all of these same purposes.

If ordinary folks in Africa can make cave paintings, so can you. Think of an event with or without animals that you want to commemorate or think of a decorating theme or an animal you want to feature, like giraffes.

This snapshot of daily life in Botswana 2,000 years ago shows two men or boys herding fat-tailed sheep.

You'll need

A "cave" wall in, say, your bedroom or the garage (with parents' permission, please). If you cannot paint directly on the wall, secure a very large piece of paper, such as brown wrapping paper from the post office, on the wall with masking tape.

Water-based poster paints: red, yellow, brown, black, and white (blue is never seen in cave paintings, since there are very few easily obtainable blue pigments).

1-inch, 2-inch, and 3-inch paintbrushes

1 or 2 old stiff toothbrushes

Bucket for water

Several jars or large cans for mixing paint or cleaning brushes

1. Don't sketch out your idea for a scene on a small piece of paper beforehand. Cave painters didn't have that luxury, and the resulting painting will be more spontaneous and interesting if you don't. In fact, don't

even make a sketch on the wall or large paper. Just do it!

2. After you've thought about your scene, start at one end and paint. Use one color at a time. Add a second color on top of the first, but don't get too fancy. For example, you might draw a white horse shape first, let it dry, and then add black stripes for a zebra. Don't make too many details. People, as you can see from the examples are almost always drawn as stick figures. Although you are deliberately trying to create an ancient look to your painting, use contemporary images if you want to, like a pickup truck or a motorcycle.

3. You may want to sign the painting by adding one or two negative images of your own

hand. Cave painters did this by taking a watery mixture of pigment into their mouths, placing their hands on the wall, then spitting a fine spray over their hands. It's too dangerous and messy to do that with your poster paint, but you can substitute with the toothbrush technique. Dip the old toothbrush into a watered-down solution of the color you want to spray, and shake it a bit over the paint pot to remove excess paint. Put your hand on the wall, point the brush at the hand, about six inches away, with the bristles facing upward under the thumb of the free hand. Run your thumb gently over the bristles from front to back to create the spray. Keep your hand in place on the wall

and repeat until you are happy with the amount of sprayed color. Wash your hands under lots of running water immediately when done.

These elephants and the people celebrating below them were carved into rock about 10,000 years ago.

Gorge in Tanzania enjoys several prosperous years and grows quite large. A bigger group of humans is more likely to have disagreements between the members because there are so many competing interests among the individuals of the group. Two brothers both admire the same woman who has wandered in from another valley. Perhaps her family was attacked and killed by raiders, and she escaped.

The younger brother is angry at his older brother and decides to leave the family. One night, he convinces the new woman and his younger brother to join him. He grabs a couple of new hand axes (see sidebar on page 62) and moves with them out of the crater into a cave in a neighboring valley. He sets up his own camp and raises his own family.

Multiply this scenario by thousands over thousands of years, and there are families spread all across Africa, in fact, all over the world.

Family Resemblances

In the beginning, people looked very much the same. African Eve and her family were short, slender, and dark-skinned. The rest of the people on earth (there were no people anywhere but Africa) looked similar to African Eve and her family. But, after tens of thousands of years of migration, people settled in different parts of Africa (and the rest of the world) and started to look different.

How did this happen? Let's return to our two brothers. The great-great-great- (and so on) grand-children of the first brother have wide, flat noses and very dark skin, like their great-great-great- (and so on) grandfather. Ten thousand years later, someone might tell a friend, "You'll recognize Odiambo from western Kenya. He has a typical round Luo face with a great smile."

The descendants of the second brother, who had brown skin and a rather pointed nose, look more like him. And the same ten thousand years later we might say, "There's Fara, from Addis Ababa in Ethiopia. She looks tall and statuesque."

Over time, climate and food supply affect the way humans look. The descendants of groups that settled in hot, dry country on the desert's edge became tall and lean like the Tuareg in Mali and the Maasai in Tanzania. A larger skin surface helps the body dispel heat, and long legs are good for running after stray cattle and chasing enemies. Short, chubby offspring would probably die of heat stress before having a chance to reproduce. Goodbye to short, chubby genes in Maasai lands. In contrast, the people who migrated to the far south of the continent became rather plump. The months of June and July can get pretty cold there, and the extra weight acts as insulation.

Early Africans who established homes in the jungles stayed small and agile, such as the Mbuti pygmies in the Congo's Ituri Forest. They can slip through thick underbrush and climb trees quickly to escape large animals or catch small ones. A person as tall as a Maasai might get caught in the underbrush when trying to flee an angry buffalo. Bye-bye to tall genes in the Congo forest.

Humans hardly ever become loners like rhinos or leopards. In fact, the main characteristic of human behavior is that we tend to live in social groups, like chimpanzees or elephants. Those groups that settled way out of Africa—in Europe, China, the Pacific Islands, and eventually North and South America—became taller or shorter, lighter or darker, or fatter or thinner based on how their bodies adapted to climate and terrain. Basically, though, we're all the same under the skin.

I tell my students, it's not difficult to identify with somebody like yourself, somebody next door who looks like you. What's more difficult is to identify with someone you don't see, who's very far away, who's a different color, who eats a different kind of food. When you begin to do that, then literature is really performing its wonders.

—Chinua Achebe, Nigerian novelist

Clans and Tribes

The smallest social group of people or animals is referred to as a "nuclear family," which usually includes a mother, a father, kids, and maybe a grandparent or two. The next level is referred to as the "extended family" or clan. This group includes other relatives, like aunts, uncles, cousins, and other men and women who have come into the family through marriage.

There may also be other clans that live in the same region. As neighbors trade or negotiate to share resources, common language develops. This is how ethnic groups, or tribes, form. Most major ethnic groups live in more than one country because the colonial rulers drew boundaries without much regard to the groupings of people. Today Tuaregs live in Algeria and Mali, Maasai in Kenya and Tanzania, and the San in Botswana, South Africa, Namibia, and Angola.

What is a tribe or ethnic group? A group of people, many of whom may be related, who live in the same general area and live off the products of a shared ecosystem, or did for much of their history. They speak the same language and practice a common set of rituals. They agree on a code of conduct; that is, they make up rules about what the right behavior is and is not. They also agree on what to do if someone in the group breaks the rules.

A tribe usually has a leader who is chosen by members of the tribe because he or she is particularly intelligent or wise, or perhaps good at getting people to work together. In some tribes, the job of leader is passed from father to son, a kind of "royal family." In others, a group of elders makes decisions for the tribe. Occasionally, tribal leaders take control by force, but usually they do not remain in power very long.

The leader's job is to organize the growing community, help keep the peace, act as a judge in disputes, exploit shared resources, and lead fights against a common enemy. His or her biggest and probably toughest job is making decisions. If there are 1,000 people in an ethnic group, the chances that they all agree on any topic are very small.

Historically there has been a division of labor in the tribe. Some people were good at making hand axes, so others let them do it. Others were deadeye spear throwers, so they were in the front lines on a hunt. The woman who was good at curing skins may have gotten first choice of a piece of antelope if she offered to tan the hide. Modern societies work pretty much the same, only bartering is more rare and the exchange of money more common.

Early Civilizations

Africa is rich in human history because it has been inhabited by people for so long. In fact, it could be said that Africa has more history than any other continent. The ancestors of everyone living on earth today can be traced back to the African savannas of several million years ago. This is one reason why Africa holds another record: more spoken languages than any other continent, around 1,300 of them.

In colonial times, Europeans were fond of describing black Africans as "primitive savages." In fact, Africa has a rich history of highly organized kingdoms and city-states. A city-state is the name of the form of government in which a small country

that is ruled by one important city. Rome, Athens, and Venice were all ancient city-states.

In central Africa, the Great Zimbabwe (zim-BOB-weh) kingdom was a well-organized city-state over 800 years ago. Today, the kingdom's center is only a 200-acre ruin in the country now named after it, but in its heyday, the city was home to 18,000 inhabitants and was the center of a great inland empire ruled by the Karanga (kah-RAHN-gah) people.

The Great Zimbabwe is the largest of many dry-stone ruins with complex water drainage systems that are scattered across Zimbabwe and Mozambique. The oldest ones date from the eighth century A.D. The Great Zimbabwe was built with very large stones and, amazingly, no mortar to hold the stones together. This is called dry-stone building and requires great skill. A building contractor was asked to estimate what it would take to build the Great Zimbabwe in the modern world. He reckoned it would take 84 laborers two years to put the 50,000 tons of stone in place, and, with all the necessary dry-stone skilled laborers, it would cost about $6 million.

The Great Zimbabwean economy was based mainly on cattle. They also smelted gold and traded it on the shores of the Indian Ocean for glass beads and porcelain from Persia and China. Copper coins and birds carved in soapstone have been found in the ruins. The city-state was occupied until the 17th century.

What happened to the Great Zimbabwe? Mysteriously, no human remains have been found in the ruins. After several centuries of dense occupation,

Weathermen

If a drought has lingered a long time, Kikuyu (key-KOO-you) elders engage in a ritual that they believe will bring rain. They lead a white goat to the foot of a particular Mugumu (moo-GOO-moo) fig tree that has been visited for generations. There they slaughter the goat and beat its entrails against the tree. The elders then light a fire and cook and share the goat meat among them. They keep one choice piece aside, which they bury at the foot of the tree as an offering to Ngai (nn-GUY), their name for God and a word close in meaning to "sky" and "rain." According to the Kikuyu beliefs, it should then rain in a short while.

Make the First Wind Instrument

This is an advanced activity for kids who are handy with tools. Even for the experienced, adult supervision is required!

The desire to make music is a very ancient impulse, rooted deep in the human brain. Some people with brain damage who have lost the ability to speak can still sing and chant. That's because the music-making part of the brain, which is close to the brain stem, arose from a much older physical development than the formal language part of the brain, which is closer to the outside. About 50,000 years ago, perhaps a hunter-gatherer was loafing around one day and started idly blowing down a hollow grass stem or piece of bamboo. He or she made a tooting noise, which sounded like whistling. After another few thousand years of fiddling with the stem, the first flute was made. It was probably similar to a modern recorder, and you can make one, too.

Adult supervision required

You'll need

1-foot length of bamboo, about 1 inch in diameter (available at a garden shop)

Tape measure

Pencil

Saw

Hand drill with ¹⁄₁₆-inch and ¼-inch bits

Pocketknife

Wood file

Large cork, like that from a bottle of wine (try a restaurant, or ask your parents).

1. Choose a section of bamboo that looks strong and is not split. With a tape measure and pencil, mark a distance of three inches above a node (the thick, hard, knoblike bump between each section of the bamboo) and 10 inches below the node. Saw at the two places you measured. Saw carefully, particularly when getting most of the way through the section; that's when the bamboo can split.
2. Use a drill, pocketknife, and file to make or enlarge the hole through the node. It should be as large as you can make it.

3. Make the mouthpiece by carefully whittling the bamboo section above the node to create a 45-degree angle. Soften the sharp edges with the wood file.
4. Try to insert the cork into the mouthpiece end to see how much bamboo you will need to whittle off to make it fit. Use the file to remove a little at a time until the cork will fit snugly, but do not stick it in yet. Shave some of the cork off what will be the top side at an angle that matches the one you have cut into the bamboo. Use the saw (or carefully use your pocketknife) to make two lengthwise cuts about ⅛ inch apart in the top (longer) side of the cork. Carefully dig out the space between the cuts until you have a groove running the whole length of the cork about one inch deep.

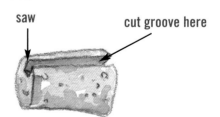

saw   cut groove here

5. The square intake airhole will be cut in the top, just above the node. Mark four spots centered on the top axis of the recorder. They should be ¼ of an inch apart top to bottom and about ½ of an inch apart side to side, across the curve of the bamboo. Draw a line between each pair of up-down holes. Drill a ¹⁄₁₆-inch hole in each spot. Drill two or three holes along the line between the up-down holes. Then, carefully saw a line between the two top and the two bottom holes. Be careful not to saw too deeply beyond the holes on the side. You may need to chip away a little with the small blade of your pocketknife to clean up the saw cuts to the holes. You should then be able to push gently on the little bamboo bridge that remains in the air hole and see it snap through to the inside of the recorder. Shake it out and clean up the edges of the air hole with your knife or the file.

6. Back to the mouthpiece: Insert the cork with the shaved angle matching that of the mouthpiece and the groove on the top. See that it fits snugly, and see if you can blow air freely through the unfinished mouthpiece. If not, remove it by poking a stick in from the other end and clean up the groove. If air passes freely and there are no leaks, finish

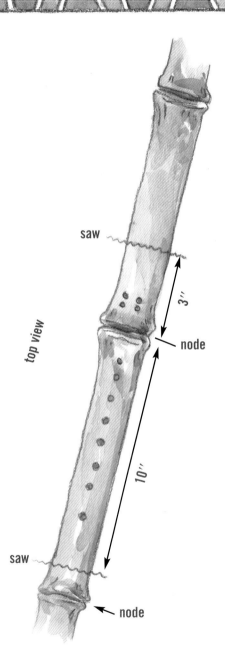

top view

saw

3"

node

10"

saw

node

the mouthpiece by smoothing down any cork that sticks out beyond the 45-degree angle with the pocketknife and file.

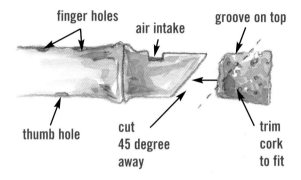

finger holes air intake groove on top

thumb hole cut 45 degree away trim cork to fit

7. Finally, make the finger holes. Mark a straight line along the top axis of the bamboo with a pencil. Then, measuring from the air hole, mark off eight holes one inch apart. For the thumbhole, on the underside of the bamboo, measure two inches from the node, and make a mark. Then, carefully—drilling slowly to avoid splitting the bamboo—drill nine clean ¼-inch holes on your marks. Clean up the hole edges with your pocketknife's small blade.

8. Play your recorder! You will need to get a feel for how gently or firmly to blow in the mouthpiece and where to position your fingers. Make up a song with your instrument.

the ecological damage around the city from cutting trees, overgrazing, and heavily cultivating the soil may have been so great that the people had to go farther and farther away to get food and fuel. Even today, certain common tree species will not grow in the area. One of Africa's periodic droughts probably came along just then, and enough was enough—the inhabitants of the Great Zimbabwe just packed their things and moved out.

The Great Zimbabwe: a great civilization long ago.

Hunting and Gathering

The African professor Ali Mazrui once wrote, "The rural world of Africa is divided between lovers of land and lovers of animals." But both farmers and herders have their roots in the ancient world of hunting and gathering, which is still the way of life of a few tribes. They live in much the same way as African Eve and African Adam must have lived.

Help me. See me. I am hungry.
See that I am sending my children into the bush.
Let them find an animal.
If not a living animal then at least a dead one
Which they can pick up and carry home,
So that I and my family can live for a day.

—!Kung Bushman prayer

Imagine a Western kid dropped off on the edge of the Kalahari Desert with only the clothes on his or her back, a knife, flint and steel for making a fire, a hollow ostrich shell for carrying water, a hardwood stick for digging, and perhaps a bow and arrow. Could the kid survive? The San Bushmen of the Kalahari in Botswana can, and they have done so for as long as anyone can remember.

Hunter-gatherer must have been the very first job description. Hunter-gatherers like the San are constantly on the move, so they don't eat all the wild animals or dig up all the roots in one place.

In the Kalahari today, small San groups live by the bow and arrow, the spear, and the snare. The San believe that a man who has not killed an animal with a bow and arrow remains a child. So San kids start practicing and participating in hunts when they are as young as six years old. The men go out hunting a lot, but they often come back empty handed. So they eat what the earth provides: plants, insects, rodents, reptiles, and birds. San women do more gathering than the men and provide the group with two and a half times more food.

San Bushmen often turn social events into religious experiences.

Because total cooperation among members of the group is so important to the group's survival, they have developed a society without individual ownership of property. It's as if a Western kid's mountain bike belonged to all of his or her friends, who could use it whenever they wanted to. The San also have complicated rules to ensure that everyone gets a share of a kill or foraging expedition. For instance, the old man who made the arrow is entitled to a part of the antelope the arrow killed, and the woman who supplied the bag gets a proportion of the berries it brings back, no matter who filled it.

Each family group has agreed-upon rights over certain areas of the Kalahari. These agreements are important during the dry season when food is scarce and the only water available is found in the spongy roots that the San dig up with sticks. San kids learn to throw sticks very accurately to knock down nuts from mangetti (man-GET-ee) trees. The nutritious nuts are a staple food of the San.

From the Western point of view, the Sans' life appears to be very tough. But if times are good, like during the rains, hunter-gatherers work only two to three days a week in order to keep themselves well fed. That leaves long stretches for cultural activities like making music, socializing, and telling stories. Acting out a story becomes a dance as women chant and clap. The men dance and hyperventilate (breathe fast and deep) until they work themselves into a kind of trance that they believe provides wisdom and strength.

So why aren't there more hunter-gatherers left today? It's not as though hunter-gatherers eagerly gave up this lifestyle to take up the hard work of pastoralists or farmers (see below). Those sensible enough to want to stay hunter-gatherers have been forced out of all good grazing land and farmland by other peoples. Look at what happened to the Native Americans in North America. Modern hunter-gatherers survive in only a few scattered areas that are useless for agriculture, such as the deserts, some rainforests, and the Arctic.

Pastoralism

Pastoralism refers to a way of making a living through raising herds of livestock that began in ancient times. Hunter-gatherers probably started domesticating dogs about 12,000 years ago. About 9,000 years ago, some clever hunter-gatherers dis-

Play the Oldest Board Game in the World

In this activity, you will make a simple *mankala* board, learn the basic rules, and play the game with a friend. Once you get the hang of it, you can play according to the rules of national variations of the game.

Mankala is the oldest board game in the world. Africans have been playing it for more than 3,000 years. The basic *mankala* board has two rows with six circles each and one circle at each end. Each player owns the row in front of him or her and the *mankala* on the right. Four pebbles are placed in each of the 12 holes in the two rows. The *mankalas* are left empty to start with. The players move stones from hole to hole according to the rules below.

You'll need

Scissors

1 empty (one dozen) egg carton

Paintbrush and paints in various colors (optional)

2 small bowls or cups

48 small pebbles (or other small round objects, such as dried beans)

1. Using the scissors, cut the lid off the egg carton. You may want to decorate it with the paints. You now have a *mankala* board.

2. Place one small bowl or cup at each end of the board. These are called *mankala*s.

3. Find an opponent. The board and cups should be placed between you. Your *mankala* is on your right; your opponent's *mankala* is on your left.

4. Put four stones in each of the 12 small holes.

5. Flip a coin to decide who moves first, then follow the rules below.

General Rules

Player 1 starts by scooping up all the stones from one of his or her small bowls. (Never start from a

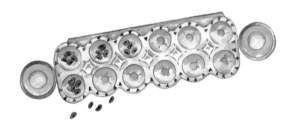

mankala or from any of the opponent's six bowls). Player 1 drops one stone into the next egg cup on the right, one stone into the second

cup on the right, and continues around the board (left to right, counterclockwise) until he or she has no more stones. If Player 1 reaches his or her own *mankala*, he or she drops a stone into it. Players do not drop stones into their opponents' *mankalas*; they skip them and continue around the board dropping stones, one at a time, until they run out of stones. If the last stone in any turn lands in an empty bowl, that player picks up the stone, plus all of the stones in the opponent's cup immediately opposite the bowl that was empty, and puts them all into the player's *mankala*. Players take turns moving. At the end of the game, players count the stones in their *mankalas*—the player with the most stones wins.

There are many different variations of the game—Egyptian, Ethiopian, Nigerian, etc. If you are interested, you can find them on the Web. Search on Google (www.google.com) for "*mankala* rules."

covered that instead of dashing around trying to catch and kill antelopes, it was a much easier to catch and domesticate them—to tame the wild animals and train them to be obedient. The first domesticated cattle were closely related to buffalo.

When a hunter kills and eats an animal, the animal is gone forever. The tribe may be able to make some useful tools out of the bones and horns and fashion a roof for the hut or a sleeping mat out of the skin, but that's the last service that particular animal will provide. In contrast, if a tribe keeps herds of animals, it's a bit like keeping money in the bank and living off the interest, rather than spending it all at once. Herders care for their animals by leading them to areas with good grass and plentiful water, by plucking disease-carrying ticks off them, and by building a corral to protect them from predators.

In exchange for care and protection, cows provide milk, blood, and occasionally meat, a luxury that is affordable when a herder knows that the well-fed and contented herd will produce more calves for the family. But milk was the key to the success and growth of pastoralism. Early pastoralists discovered that milk from herbivores would help their kids grow strong and healthy and take a large burden from nursing mothers. Drinking milk is an efficient way for animals (such as humans) who cannot digest grass to get nourishment from it indirectly. Adults also benefit from milk products like butterfat and yogurt. The development of a milk culture evolved

Maasai kids look after their father's cattle.

as human bodies adapted to break down and absorb the beneficial calcium and sugars in milk.

Pastoralism is a common way of life in most parts of the drier areas of Africa where there is not enough rain to support reliable agriculture. Because grass is a seasonal vegetation and the cattle herds eat a lot in one place, pastoralists are always on the move, chasing green grass across the countryside. Pastoralists, therefore, are nomadic, meaning they follow seasonal migration routes from place to place and back again as the rains and grasses come and go.

Pastoralists herd different species of domestic stock together depending on the rainfall and local

Build a Maasai Bivouac Shelter

Make a shelter in your own backyard. In this activity you will build a temporary Maasai hut out of sticks and grass.

During the dry season, Maasai kids as young as 10 years old have to lead their family's herds of cattle, sheep, and goats many miles from the family corral to find grass and water. Sometimes, brothers and sisters spend a couple of nights outside with the animals. They need to build a *boma* (BOW-ma) for the animals and a shelter for themselves. *Boma* is Swahili for "enclosure" or "corral." The *boma* is typically made out of thorny branches cut from acacia trees and placed on the ground facing outward, toward prowling lions or hyenas.

The shelter for herders is a little hut made out of sticks and grass. It's very flimsy, made to last for only a couple of days. You can make one for yourself and your friends to take shelter in!

Adult supervision required

You'll need

A flat, wide space at least six feet around with loose soil

30 flexible sticks, 5–6 feet long (make sure you get permission to collect or cut these down)

Saw

Pocketknife

Roll of twine

Scissors

Pile of long cut grass *or* a bale of wheat straw *or* several old blankets or pieces of canvas

1. Find a site for your shelter. It should be flat with soil that is not too hard so you can push sticks into the soil. Maasai kids would also be careful not to make the bivouac too close to a river in case of a flash flood and not directly under a tree in case of lightning or rainfall, which will continue to drip from the tree onto the shelter even after the rain storm is over. You won't build a *boma*, but think about where you could locate a small corral about 20 feet in diameter, which would include your shelter. Be sure to get permission to build your shelter from the landowner or from your parents if you are going to use your backyard.

2. Trim the sticks so they are all about the same length. Sharpen the fat end with your pocketknife.

3. With a stick, draw a circle in the soil, about six feet in diameter (about three paces). Push the fat end of the sticks firmly into the soil along the edge of the circle, about one foot apart. Leave a two-foot space between one pair of sticks: this will become the opening to the bivouac. You should have used about 15 sticks. Number the sticks as in the diagram, 1 to 15, with a stick in the dirt.

two sticks and the loop you've already made, keeping a bit of the free end of the loop sticking out. Wrap the long end of the twine around the sticks and loop neatly until you get to the closed end of the loop, leaving a bit of it protruding. Now you've made the lash. To finish, pass the working end through the protruding closed end of the loop. With the working end in one hand and the "loop end" in the other, pull the ends away from each other until the closed end of the loop tucks up under the lashing.

Tie or lash them in this order: 2 and 9, 7 and 14, 4 and 12, 3 and 11, 5 and 13. Then, finish off the opening sticks 1 and 10, 6 and 15. That leaves number 8, which you can stretch over the top of all sticks and leave protruding over the opening. It will be handy for putting a cloth over if it should rain.

4. Tie or lash 14 nearly opposite sticks together in the middle at the top of the bivouac, using the numbers on the diagram.

Lashing means binding two or more things together with many turns of string or rope. Here's a simple lash for two overlapping sticks. Cut an 18-inch length of twine and hold it between your teeth. Hold the two overlapping sticks together with your right hand (reverse if you are left-handed). Make a 2–3-inch loop in one end of the twine, hold its open end under your thumb, and lay the loop along the overlapping sticks. With your free hand, start turning the twine around the

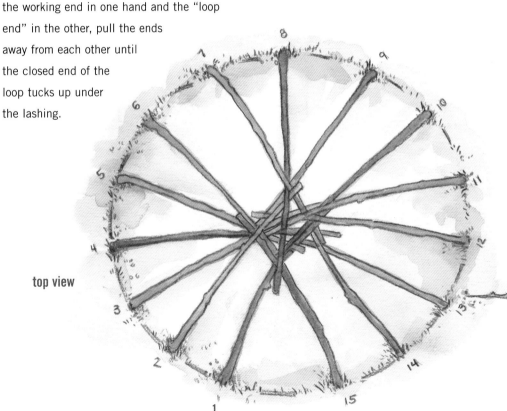

top view

6. Now cover the structure as best you can. If you have long grass, start at the bottom of the horizontal sticks, take a big handful of grass, and bend about five inches of it over the stick toward the inside and tie it with a loop of twine. If you run out of grass, finish the top with an old blanket or piece of canvas or plastic. Maasai kids would probably do the same if nightfall were coming.

7. If you dare (and have permission!) and the weather looks good, throw some grass or straw on the ground and spend the night. Maasai kids would wrap themselves up in their *shuka*s (SHOE-kah), the blankets they wear all day, but you can use a sleeping bag.

5. To strengthen the structure, tie or lash the remaining sticks around the outside of the structure so you have at least three rows of horizontal sticks.

vegetation. In good grassland, cows are the best bet: they produce lots of milk and meat. In drier country with shrubby vegetation, smaller sheep and goats do well. Some pastoralists have herds of both cows and "shoats" (that's what researchers call mixed herds of sheep and goats when you cannot tell one species from another as you are counting them from a light airplane). Pastoralists rely on cows during good rains and "shoats" during bad rains.

In really dry country on the edge of the desert, the camel is the beast of choice. Camels provide milk and eventually meat when they become too old to be useful. You cannot imagine how tough meat from an old camel is until you've eaten it. The main use of camels in desert country is for transportation. They can be ridden for long distances without having to stop to drink water. They also have special desert adaptations, like large, flat feet for walking on sand and nostrils that can squeeze shut in a sandstorm.

The Maasai are pastoralists who live in Kenya and Tanzania. Their social structure includes a fierce warrior class of young males between the life stages of puberty and fatherhood. Traditionally, the warriors were necessary to defend their own herds and steal cattle from neighboring tribes. Maasai folklore holds that at the beginning of time the great god Ngai decreed that all the cattle on earth belong to the Maasai. Therefore, the Maasai believe that if they take cattle from other people, it's not really stealing because the cattle belonged to them

What's That in the Milk Jug?

According to Zulu legend, there is a mythical lizard-like being called an *imbulu* (eem-BOO-loo) that steals milk at night from the family milk jug, the *ithunga* (ee-THUNG-ah). The best defense against the *imbulu* is believed to be this: leave a little milk in the bottom of the jug. To reach the milk, the *imbulu* has to climb far into the jug, which is slippery on the inside. The not-so-bright *imbulu* then slips, falls into the milk, and drowns. The legend doesn't say what happens in the morning. Hopefully, the family dumps out the drowned *imbulu* and washes out the jug before adding fresh milk.

The Maasai in East Africa have a distinctive way of preparing and serving milk, which is a staple in their diet. They scrape out the inside of a large gourd and use the flesh and seeds for making soup. Then they drop hot coals into the gourd's narrow mouth and shake them around long enough to scour the inside without burning through the gourd. When the coals and ashes are dumped out, the gourd is ready to use as a milk container. It's called a "calabash" in English or *e-mpukuri* (EH-mm-poo-KOO-ree) in Maa, the language of the Maasai. The Maasai women squeeze milk from a cow's teat directly into the calabash, push a wooden plug into the top, and then let it sit at room temperature for a day or so. When the milk has fermented, or soured, it is drunk as a slightly smoky-tasting yogurt.

in the first place. Today, African governments do not agree with this traditional notion, and a cattle rustler is locked up as quickly as a car thief.

Because cows are like money in the bank to the Maasai and because cows are the basis of their economy, they keep as many as possible. Sometimes this causes problems during droughts, when grass gets overgrazed and cattle die of starvation. Only then will Maasai become hunters. They feel that most wild herbivores, with the possible exception of the eland, are inferior to cattle as food. This is why some of the best wildlife areas in eastern Africa are in

Make a Model Maasai Nkang

Have you ever made or seen a diorama? In this activity you will build a small model of a typical scene in Africa.

The cattle-herding pastoralists of southern and East Africa may settle for one or two years in one location if the grazing is good. For long-term encampments, the Maasai of Kenya and Tanzania construct an oblong, low-domed hut, about six yards long and five feet wide, from closely woven frames of thin sticks and saplings. The frames are arranged in a circle around the cattle enclosure, or *boma*, packed with leaves, and plastered over with cattle dung, which is good insulation and acts as a deterrent to termites. The *boma* boundary is made of thorn bushes to keep the livestock in and the lions and hyenas out. The whole settlement, basically the village of one family group, is called an *nkang* (nn-KONG). In this activity, you will make a small-scale model *nkang*.

A Maasai *nkang* from the air.

78

You'll need

Scissors

Large cardboard box

Pencil

A common pin or needle

2 or 3 packets of wooden toothpicks

Rubber cement or contact glue

Plasticine (a plastic "clay" used for models; use
earth colors if possible: browns, reds, yellows)

Masking tape

A small pile of one-inch bits of woody shrubbery,
snapped or clipped from a hedge

Green wrapping paper or tissue

A few small stones

Red wrapping paper or tissue

1. Cut the box at its seams so the cardboard lays
   flat. Spread the sides until you have a stable
   working surface of about 2½ by 2 feet.

2. Use the illustration on this page to sketch out
   the outline of your huts. There will be four or
   five huts (one for each of the three wives and
   her young children, one for the elder who is the
   family leader, and one for visiting elder sons,
   married daughters, or guests). There may also
   be a small enclosure inside for young livestock.
   Very young calves are kept in the huts at night.

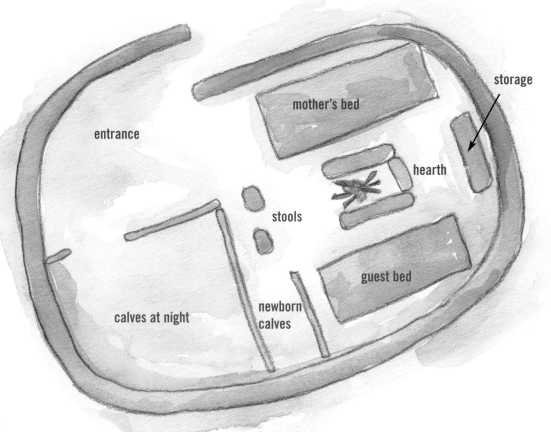

3. If you make the entire *nkang* about 24 inches long by 18 inches wide, and each hut about three inches long, you will have a model on a scale of 1:72; that is, one inch on your model represents 72 inches on the ground. So, your three-inch huts will represent huts 216 inches (3 x 72 = 216) or six yards long.

4. To make the huts, start with the upright poles. Take the pin and make a line of tiny holes in the cardboard about one-fourth of an inch apart along the outlines of each hut on your plan. Make the doors open to the inside of the circle of huts. With a toothpick, spread a thin line of glue along the line of holes. Break a large number of toothpicks in half and stick them into the holes. Line them up before the glue dries, and you have a row of stakes, much like the ones the Maasai women cut and collect to make their huts.

5. Next, make the roofs of the huts. From a spare piece of cardboard, cut out a roof for each hut just larger than the group of toothpicks. Put a dab of glue on the protruding ends of the six tallest toothpicks and a dab of plasticine on the ends of the six shortest (to make up for length differences), line them up once again, and set the roof on top. Let dry.

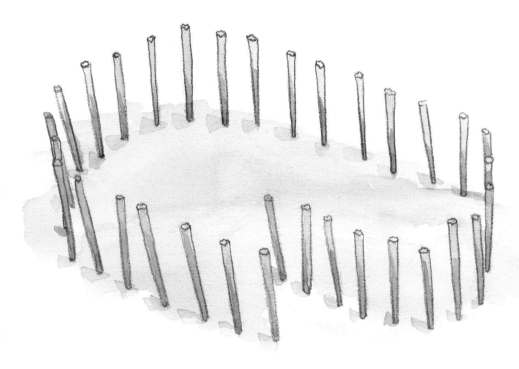

You can calculate the height a 2½-inch toothpick broken in half represents on the scale models, and when stuck into the cardboard, the toothpicks approximate the height of the low Maasai huts: a tall man—and most Maasai are tall—has to stoop to enter.

6. Plaster the huts. First tear off 6- to 8-inch lengths of masking tape, and use them to cover the gaps between the toothpicks. Then, warm up some brown plasticine by placing it in your hand, hold the roof steady, and apply it to the masking tape on the sides of the huts. You can cover the roofs with a thin layer

as well to give the appearance that the whole thing is covered in a plaster of mud and cow dung.

7. Make the *boma*. Using the same technique as above, make a more widely spaced fence of toothpicks along the outline of the *boma*, about ½–¾ inch apart. Leave a one-inch gap by each hut. Stick the bits of clipped shrubbery between the toothpicks, with the bushy parts out. Maasai would use thorn bushes to repel hyenas and lions. You can leave the one-inch gap open during the day as a quick gate to each hut, but it must be closed with thick branches during the night. The number of gates in an *nkang* is usually equal to the number of women married to one husband.

8. Decorate your *nkang*. You may want to add a couple of trees just inside the *boma*, and some cows and sheep if you have access to an old farmyard play set. You can make a tree by sticking one end of a toothpick through a crumple of green wrapping or tissue paper. A few ½-inch stones arranged in a circle give the elder a place to have a discussion with visitors.

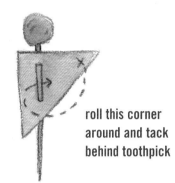

roll this corner around and tack behind toothpick

You can even add a couple of Maasai. Cut one-inch by one-inch corners from a scrap of red paper. Stick a half toothpick through the narrowest point of the triangle, curl one base angle inside, and poke the toothpick out through the other base angle. Stick a glob of brown plasticine on the top end, and you have a stylized rendition of a warrior or an elder. Use the other half of the toothpick to give him a spear to lean on.

Bush School

Older, traditional Maasai herders have very different ideas about school than most North American parents. For the Maasai, the most important job is ensuring the well-being of the family's herds of cows, sheep, and goats. So they assign the important task of shepherding to the most intelligent kids. These kids are the ones who can quickly learn the identities of all the cows: which have calves or are about to give birth, which give more milk, which are important to various family members, and so on. These kids must also be adept at finding water and good grazing areas and reading signs in the wild that suggest the herder should avoid trouble spots and dangerous animals. The old-timers think that these kids should not fritter away their talents in a schoolroom—better to have kids working in the bush tending the herds.

What happens to the less clever kids? They are sent to school! This is one reason why only about one in three Maasai children attend school. As a result, over 90 percent of Maasai can neither read nor write.

Illiteracy is costly and dangerous. In colonial times, the almost totally illiterate Maasai signed over their best grazing lands to the British. Today, the existing grazing land they own can barely support their growing population. Also, it is easier for the literate neighboring tribes to cheat them in trade, business, and land deals.

In Tanzania, which used to have one of the highest literacy rates in Africa, a head teacher lost his job when parents complained he was helping too many children pass the equivalent of sixth grade. What's wrong with that, you wonder? If the kids passed, they would want to go on to high school, which the parents could not afford and did not think would support the community.

But some younger Maasai are trying to change things. Peter Lowara is a Maasai social worker in Kenya. He says, "My father hated me because he thought I was not his, so he chased me off to school. It was terrible—I felt like I had no prospects." So Peter has started a project for Maasai kids called *Osiligi*, which means "hope" in Maa. Every afternoon, young herders gather in the shade of an acacia tree to learn to read and write in English and Swahili, as well as to calculate basic arithmetic problems from blackboards nailed to tree trunks. Volunteer teachers also teach them the basics of Maasai culture, hygiene, and animal husbandry. In regular government schools the kids would be forced to learn about crops like coffee and vegetables that do not even grow in the surrounding dry grasslands.

After learning the basics, perhaps 1 in 20 of the Maasai students will abandon herding to go to regular schools. From there, they will have a better prospect of securing jobs in other parts of Kenya. The kids who stay with the family herds can now at least read the English instructions on packets of veterinary drugs or hold their own against Swahili-speaking livestock traders to get a fair price.

What happens to the herds during the bush school period? The kids from the regular school use their afternoon breaks to take turns looking after the herds. Maybe one day—hopefully soon—all students will all have the same chance to learn.

Dinka herders with their beloved cattle.

Maasai territory: the Serengeti in Tanzania and the Amboseli and Laikipia (lie-KIP-ee-ah) in Kenya.

The Dinka people of southern Sudan are one of the last tribes in Africa who practice a purely ancient way of living. There are nearly three million of them. They live in a low-lying region where the Nile wanders slowly north to the Sahara Desert. The steamy edges of the Sudd swamp are extremely hot and humid, so the Dinka quite sensibly go around naked, wearing only a decorative bead belt around their waists. That leaves their skin exposed to the serious possibility of mosquito bites, so they fill their simple huts and cattle corrals with the smoke of burning cattle dung and cover themselves with the ashes.

If it is possible to imagine, the Dinkas love their cattle even more than the Maasai love theirs. Although their cows are small and do not provide much meat when butchered, they produce milk and have been bred to have huge, spectacular horns.

Like the climate in most areas near deserts, the days are burning hot, but the nights can be very cold, particularly during the dry season when there are not many clouds to trap the heat built up during the day. It is not unusual for a Dinka child to fight an early morning chill by having a nice warm shower behind a urinating cow before beginning his milking chores.

Agriculture

Around 10,000 years ago, another bright hunter-gatherer discovered that if she replanted some of the grass seeds she had been harvesting for food, during the next rains more grass would grow in that place. That meant she wouldn't have to walk so far to harvest. And that revelation was the beginning of agricul-

Is Agriculture a Good Thing?

Although it might seem that an agricultural society is both progressive and civilized, in fact, agricultural production has been both a blessing and a curse for humans. The main advantage of producing a lot of one kind of food in one place is that a bountiful food source allows rapidly growing populations of humans to survive, and to live closer together. But agriculture in Africa has also resulted in poor nutrition, starvation, disease, and discrimination. Here's why. As agriculturalists turned to starchy crops, they abandoned the old hunter-gatherer diet that is rich in protein, vitamins, minerals, and, if hunting is good, fat. The result of consuming lots of calories mainly from crops is poor nutrition.

If a farming community depends on just one or two crops, a bad drought or plague of locusts on that crop can wipe out the entire food supply. This is why there are so many reports of starvation among people in Ethiopia, Sudan, or the area along the southern edge of the Sahara where farmers live. San hunter-gatherers, in contrast, depend on about 85 species of wild plants and numerous wild animals. No matter how bad the drought, they will always find something to eat.

Most of the worse diseases facing people today—like malaria, tuberculosis, leprosy, and cholera—first became threats to humans after the invention of agriculture. Why? People started living closer together in large numbers, in communities with unsanitary conditions. As people became even more jammed together in cities, smallpox, the bubonic plague, and measles started killing people by the millions.

Of course, Africa cannot return to hunting and gathering. Its population is far too large to support in that way. What kinds of strategies could help to overcome the deficiencies of traditional agriculture? Answering this question is Africa's challenge.

Make Cassava Chips

Cassava chips are a healthy alternative to potato chips.

Cassava is an important staple food in much of sub-Saharan Africa. In North America, the root is largely unknown and can taste quite bland to Western palates, but these cassava chips are not only quick and easy to make, they're delicious!

Adult supervision required

You'll need

A vegetable brush or other scrub brush

2–3 medium-sized cassava roots, about three inches in diameter (these can be obtained from large vegetable markets, specialty food stores, or health food stores)

Cooking knife

Potato peeler

Bowl of cold water

1 quart vegetable oil

Cooking range on a stove or a deep fryer

A sturdy, flat-bottomed 3–4-quart cooking pot with a short handle if you do not have a deep fryer

Several kitchen towels

A large sieve or deep-frying basket

Sea salt or ordinary salt

(Chile powder for the spicy variety)

1. Scrub the cassava roots with a brush under running water. Cut the ends off the cassava so that the smallest diameter of the root is not less than two inches.

2. With a vegetable knife or potato peeler, slice as many thin slices off the ends as you can. They should look like raw potato chips. Put them in a bowl of cold water to soak for about an hour.

3. Pour the oil into the cooking pot and heat to 370 degrees (if you don't have a thermometer that can be used in very hot oil, you can tell oil has reached 370 degrees if it browns a one-inch cube of bread in 60 seconds). **Be very careful of the hot oil splattering or spilling**.

4. While the oil is heating, remove the cassava slices from the water and spread them out on kitchen towels to dry. Pat them dry on the top with more towels. It is important that they aren't excessively wet as the water will cause the hot oil to bubble.

5. When the oil reaches the correct temperature, use a large sieve or deep-frying basket to carefully lower two handfuls of the cassava slices into the hot oil.

6. Let cook until the slices become light golden brown. Lift the basket carefully out of the oil, let excess oil drain off for a few moments, and then dump the cooked chips onto more kitchen towels to remove excess oil.

7. Wait until the hot oil has returned to the proper temperature (it will cool a bit during cooking), and then add another batch of slices and repeat until all are cooked. If the oil starts smoking, either it is too hot or it needs to be replaced with fresh oil.

8. Sprinkle the chips lightly with salt. A spicy variation can be made by adding a couple of pinches of chili powder to the salt. Let cool, and serve to friends and family with a hearty "*karibu!*" (welcome).

ture (although there is some evidence that people had been controlling the distribution of roots and tubers in southern Africa as long as 70,000 years ago).

Today, the staple foods of millions of people in western and northern Africa are millet and sorghum, which are cultivated grasses that grow to eight feet tall and produce grains that look to Westerners like birdseed.

The Portuguese brought maize (a grain that Americans call corn) and cassava into Africa from South America in the 1500s. Maize was intended to be a cheap food source that could be used to keep slaves alive until they could be shipped to their destination. Maize is now the staple food of millions of people in eastern and southern Africa.

Cassava or manioc is a root domesticated from a poisonous plant. Imagine how many human ancestors got sick or even died as ancient peoples figured out how to process the starchy roots. Cassava grows in all kinds of soils, at all altitudes, in wet or dry conditions, so it provides nourishment to people all over Africa (and the rest of the world). Because cassava can be grown in so many different climates, it can be cultivated on unproductive land often used by poor farmers. North American kids have probably tasted cassava in the form of tapioca pudding.

Bananas

If you were abandoned on a desert island and could only take one fruit plant with you, what should you choose? A banana plant! Bananas and their less sweet cousins, plantains, are high-energy foods and three times more productive than cereals. They are also rich in vitamin C and potassium. You cannot live on bananas alone, but one plant can grow into a banana garden that will produce a crop every year of your life (or until you get rescued from the desert island).

Bananas reproduce by vegetative means; that is, without having to rely on flowers and seeds. They put much of their growth effort into a seedless fruit that develops from female flowers that do not have to be fertilized. The banana plants make more plants by sending out side shoots from the roots. The original plant gives all its nutrition and energy to the shoots and will eventually wither and die. But, if there's a handy farmer around, he or she can pluck off the shoot and transplant it nearby so both the parent plant and the new plant will continue to grow and produce fruit. Pretty soon, you have a banana garden.

Although bananas originally came from Asia, they have been cultivated by African farmers for over 2,000 years. A banana may be just a banana to you, but in Africa, there are 60 varieties of the sweet kind and 120 types of plantains. Today, Africa produces 35 percent of the world's banana crop. In those parts of west, central, and East Africa where bananas and plantains are the main food crop, Africans eat 550 pounds per year. That's over three bananas or plantains a day. People in the United States eat an average of only one banana a week.

Bananas are the main crop of the Bantu people living around the Great Lakes in central and eastern Africa. They have 60 words for banana varieties and another 40 terms to describe parts of the plants or ways of preparing them for food or brewing them for banana beer. Does that seem strange to you? Consider this. For Swahili speakers, a dog is just an *mbwa* (um-BWAH). They would find it very strange that North Americans have words for so many different types of dogs: cocker spaniels, German shepherds, Irish setters, toy poodles, and so on.

Some Tasty Banana Recipes

Bananas make great side dishes and even desserts. Impress your family and friends with these easy and tasty recipes.

Banana Dhow

Dhow is the name for a type of ship that has sailed between the Arabian Peninsula and the East African coast for 1,000 years. Bananas were one of the first products exported to the Arab world.

Adult supervision required

You'll need

Kitchen knife

1 banana per person

Aluminum foil

1–2 tablespoons chopped dried fruit

1–2 tablespoons chocolate chips or coarsely chopped plain chocolate

1–2 tablespoons crushed cashew nuts

Grill or charcoal fire

1. For each serving, cut a V-shaped wedge lengthwise in a firm, peeled, ripe banana. Discard the wedge (or eat it!).

2. Place the banana on a piece of double-thickness aluminum foil. Fill the groove with dried fruit, chocolate chips, and crushed cashew nuts.

3. Ask an adult to prepare the grill or small charcoal fire.

4. Wrap the banana securely in the foil and cook over charcoal or under a grill for about 10 minutes.

5. After cooking, sculpt the foil into the shape of a boat. Add a paper sail on a stick. Raise the sail and serve!

Matoke

Matoke (ma-TOE-kay) are, like plantains, non-sweet bananas. They are a staple food eaten throughout eastern and central Africa.

You'll need

Oven
12 plantains, peeled
Large pot of water
½ cup lime juice
Cooking stove
Strainer
Large bowl
Small bowl

Potato masher or other utensil for mashing
1 cup coconut milk (available in a can or
    powder form)
Pinch of cayenne pepper
1 bunch fresh cilantro leaves, chopped (dry
    coriander can be used instead)
Salt and pepper
An oven-proof baking dish

1. Preheat the oven to 300 degrees.
2. Place the plantains in a large pot of water with a spoonful of lime juice and bring the water to a boil on the stove. Boil until tender.
3. Drain the plantains in a strainer and mash well in a large bowl.
4. Mix the remaining ingredients thoroughly in a small bowl and add them to the mashed plantains. If the mixture seems too thick (difficult to stir with a large spoon), add more coconut milk and lime juice. Add salt and pepper to taste.
5. Spoon into an ovenproof dish. Bake for 20 minutes.

    Serve as a side dish with any other dish with which you would normally serve mashed potatoes. A pat of butter makes them delicious.

Serves 2–3

Colonialism and Racism

For over a thousand years after the birth of Christ, Africans living in the interior of the continent lived their lives undisturbed by the developments of other civilizations across the globe. On the coasts, and especially in North Africa, the African continent was less isolated. Roman military expeditions penetrated quite far into northern Africa to bring back gold, ivory, and slaves to serve as gladiators. They even brought back elephants and other exotic animals to show off to crowds in Rome. Seafaring traders and adventurers from Europe and Arabia stopped on the coasts to get water and fruit and to conduct trade with the local people. By about A.D. 700, after the Muslim conquest of North Africa, camel caravans of Arab traders crossed the Sahara as far as Timbuktu in search of slaves and gold. Seafaring Arab traders started riding the monsoon winds to East Africa, making regular landings in Lamu (LAH-moo), Mombasa (mohm-BAH-sah), and Zanzibar.

Exploration by sea increased around the world in the 14th and 15th centuries. Cheng Ho was a Chinese military leader who had been captured as a boy and forced into the army. He distinguished himself in the military and was chosen by the emperor to explore the lands around the Indian Ocean. He reached East Africa on his fourth voyage in 1414. Envoys from Malindi (mah-LIN-dee), in what is now Kenya, went back to Beijing with Cheng Ho to present the emperor with gifts, including a live giraffe. Pieces of Chinese pottery from the Ming Dynasty have been found all along the East African coast, proving that the Chinese were trading with Africans 600 years ago.

Meanwhile, the Portuguese were busy developing a thriving trade on the west African coast. Sailing ships brought woolen cloth, cotton, silver, and carpets to Africa for the traders to exchange for exotic animal hides, honey, beeswax, civet cats (who produce a substance from their musk glands that was used in perfume making), gum arabic (a sticky resin from acacia trees used in making candies even today), fish, ostrich eggs, and, most important, gold and slaves.

In 1448 the first permanent European building was erected on Arguim Island (ahr-GHAIN) off the Mauritanian coast. It was a trading post, fort, and fishing port. Other forts and outposts quickly followed along the coastline to what was called the Gold Coast, which includes several modern countries: Liberia, Ivory Coast, Ghana, Togo, and Benin.

Wherever the Portuguese landed and established an outpost, they would erect a *padrão* (pawd-RAO), a six-foot stone cross, to mark their discovery, claim ownership, and announce the arrival of Christianity in "heathen" lands. Of course, they didn't really own the land, but the assumption among explorers and traders was "finders, keepers." Later, wars were fought between non-African countries about who owned different parts of Africa, usually without bothering to ask the Africans what they wanted or what they owned or shared.

The first Dutch colony was established at the Cape of Good Hope near the southern tip of Africa in 1652. But it took another 100 years for European governments to finance explorers and missionaries to penetrate into the heart of Africa. In the 1800s, the number of explorers, missionaries, and slave traders from Europe and the Arabian Peninsula increased, as the number of these adventurers did all over the world. Permanent settlements were set up and military personnel followed to protect the colonists and the nation's trade interests. It wasn't long before the European colonials were fighting each other.

This period in Africa's history has been called "the scramble for Africa." The time is marked by outsiders stealing Africa's riches for profit and claiming territory to increase the power of the invading country. Missionaries joined the scramble to convert Africans to Christianity or Islam, whether the Africans liked it or not. Understandably, the indigenous Africans resisted the invaders. But the invaders had guns, and they brought unknown germs. Between unfair battles and incurable sicknesses, the Africans stood little chance of repelling them.

Through force, fraud, and violence, the people of North, East, West, Central and Southern Africa were relieved of their political and economic power and forced to pay allegiance to foreign monarchs.
—Nelson Mandela

Apartheid

Apartheid (a-PART-tide, meaning "apartness" in Afrikaans) was one of the nastiest official government systems ever implemented. Under apartheid, South Africa's white minority practiced racial segregation and political and economic discrimination against people who weren't white, called "nonwhites." In some ways, it was a lot like the segregation practiced between whites and blacks in the United States until the 1960s.

Nonwhites couldn't travel freely or even go into some "whites only" areas; they were forced to live in special areas called "townships." They could only get menial jobs, and they had to use different public toilets and drinking fountains from whites. All South Africans had to carry pass cards that identified their race: white; Bantu (meaning black people, although the word really refers to the main group of languages spoken in eastern, central, and southern Africa); colored (people of mixed race); and Asian (descendents of East Indian origin).

Unlike the periods of slavery and segregation in the United States during which whites were the majority, in South Africa, there were only five million whites trying to dominate 35 million nonwhites. The South African whites believed they had the right to run the country because their ancestors had settled in South Africa 300 years before.

But domination by force can never work for long. The people being dominated will always resist and demand their rights as human beings. So, after much struggle and bloodshed, President F. W. de Klerk made apartheid illegal in 1990. In a free and fair election following the abolition of apartheid, the people of South Africa—whites included—elected Nelson Mandela (see page 127) as their first nonwhite president.

By 1885, the European powers had divided up most of the continent and decided among themselves which part "belonged" to which colonial country without regard to the rights of African inhabitants. By 1914, colonization covered nearly the whole continent.

The story of colonialism is told in many different languages because it affected so many different

Thumb Pianos

The *mbira* (mm-BEER-a) or "thumb piano" is played throughout sub-Saharan Africa and makes a beautiful, lilting sound. It's called a *kalimba* in eastern Africa and *sansa* in the Congo. There are many variations of *mbiras*, from elaborately decorated metal boxes to simple cigar boxes. A number of metal or split bamboo keys are affixed to the box in such a way that they can be plucked with the thumbs as the box is held in both hands. The box helps amplify the sound, and the length of the keys determines the pitches of the notes.

The *mbira*'s metal keys were originally smelted directly from rocks containing iron ore. Now, they may be made from just about anything—sofa springs, bicycle spokes, car seat springs, the teeth of a metal rake, or other recycled steel materials. Metal beads or curled bits of a tin can are often set on the keys between the bridge and the bridge clamp. This adds a buzz to the notes. The buzz is considered an essential part of the *mbira* sound. It clears the mind of worries to let music fill the thoughts of the performers and listeners.

Mbiras were first observed by Portugese explorers in 1586, and they spread with the slave trade to the Americas. The instrument is commonly used during festive occasions to accompany a song or dance. It also has a religious function and is used to chase off evil. The noise also serves to give buffalo an early warning of human presence, to prevent humans from surprising them and provoking an attack.

Visit the Web site http://pbskids.org/africa/piano/haveflash.html to play an *mbira* online and hear how it sounds.

people, but it's pretty much the same story around the world. The accounts often include a bit of good news and a lot of bad news.

The good news is that medicine, education, and infrastructure were imported into the colonies within a very short time, which meant that Africans were introduced to certain positive Western developments. Infrastructure is a catch-all word to describe all those things that a centralized government provides: roads, railroads, electricity, telephones, and sewage systems.

The bad news, however, goes on and on. The colonial authorities set up governments modeled on their governments back home, gave the important jobs to nationals from the colonial power, and gave the menial, unskilled, or tedious jobs to the Africans. Many Africans at that time were not accustomed to an economy based on money: they lived by bartering and sharing. The sudden offer of wages, no matter how miserable the conditions, proved attractive since it allowed them to buy things from the growing number of shops that were springing up in the wake of colonialism. At best the Africans were treated like second-class citizens; at worst they were turned into slaves.

Every effort was made to change the native Africans to make them fit the colonizers' image of civilized and cultured people. The missionaries set up churches so the newly converted Africans could worship "properly." Schools were set up to teach the English, French, or Portuguese language, along with

Western subjects. The result was that traditional ways of life were made to seem bad, and much ancient and useful knowledge was lost, including oral histories and legends, folk remedies, and tricks of survival under harsh conditions.

But, most importantly, the indigenous Africans in colonial countries were not free. They could not choose their own political leaders because the colonial powers put their own people in charge. They were not allowed to own property or live in the best neighborhoods, they could not come and go as they pleased, and they were not allowed into some public buildings.

Most African countries were under colonial rule until the 1960s. After bitter struggles, some that lasted 100 years, most African colonies became independent nations by 1968. The Belgian Congo became the Republic of the Congo in 1960; Senegal became fully independent of France in 1960; British East Africa became the independent states of Tanzania, Uganda, and Kenya between 1961 and 1963; in 1966, Lesotho and Botswana, and, in 1990, Namibia, all became independent of the Republic of South Africa. So most African states have been self-governing countries for less than 40 years.

Although an ardent nationalist, Julius Nyerere (nye-REH-reh), the first president of Tanzania, observed a positive result from colonialism: a spirit of oneness among Africans. For hundreds of years, the colonial powers were the common enemies of Africans. This unity helped African peoples across the continent, who are culturally as different from one another as the Chinese are from the Dutch, develop a growing sense of pride in being African, what Léopold Senghor (seng-GORE), the first president of Senegal, called "negritude" (see page 109).

Slavery

Forced human labor has always been attractive to people who could afford to buy slaves, sickening as we find the practice today. In Africa, by the end of the first millennium, Arab slave traders plied along the southern margin of the Sahara in west Africa. As seafaring trade increased in the 15th century, Portuguese explorers looking for gold and ivory along Africa's west coast found many locals who were also willing to supply slaves, usually captured from neighboring tribes. In only five years, between 1441 and 1446, nearly 1,000 men, women, and children where shipped off to Portugal.

But those shipments of slaves were very small compared to the shipments to come. Between 1450 and 1870, ten million Africans were shipped across the Atlantic Ocean to serve as slaves. A million or more died on the way. What started this gigantic trade? The simple answer is . . . sugar! Europeans had acquired a taste for sweetness. Sugarcane plantations in the New World could produce enough sugar to satisfy the sweet teeth of Europeans, but it took a lot of labor to plant and cut the cane fields. Slaves provided the labor at low cost.

Child Labor: Get the Facts from UNICEF

Ask a couple of friends or classmates to log on to the UNICEF Web site with you and take the child labor quiz. Here's the URL: http://www.unicef.org/voy/explore/rights/711_childlabourquiz.php

Compare your results. You'll be astonished at how many kids your age are forced to work for almost nothing at jobs that most adults would shun.

The European taste for luxury products grew to include rum (made from sugarcane), tobacco, and fine cotton clothing. Thus, the demand for slaves to work in the fields and along the coast to support the shipping trade increased. Trade in slaves was not banned in America until 1865, after the Civil War, some 30 years after slavery had been banned throughout the British Empire.

Did slavery really end with Abraham Lincoln's Emancipation Proclamation in 1863? Well, it did on paper in America, but here is an amazing fact: slavery still exists. Some experts estimate that there are as many as 30 million people enslaved worldwide today. Here's how it happens. A poor family has to borrow money to buy food or to rent more land for planting crops or to feed a milk cow or to purchase seeds to plant. If the cow dies or the crops fail in a drought, the family may not be able to pay the money back. They then have to give something of value to the moneylender. They are poor and have almost nothing of commercial value. So the unhappy parents have to give away one of their children. The moneylender will keep the child—not as a hostage, but as something of value equivalent to the debt. If the family cannot pay off the debt, which is usually the case, the child becomes a permanent possession.

Meanwhile, the child is made to work as a domestic servant in the moneylender's house or shop. He or she receives no pay at all, is given as little food as possible to keep him or her alive, sleeps in the worst part of the house, and is often beaten or sexually abused. Although there is no official bill of sale as in olden days, the child effectively grows up a slave, with no freedom of choice and no hope of rescue. Each year hundreds if not thousands of Africans are shipped out of their homelands to other parts of the continent and sometimes even to other countries to work in this kind of slavery.

Sometimes children are taken by force. Abuk Thuc Akwar is a Sudanese girl who used to live in the south of the country. When she was 13 the government militia captured her along with 24 other children. During her forced march north, she was molested, abused, and called names. She was given to a farmer who made her work all day in his sorghum fields and serve at night as his wife. In another part of the country, Fahl Ould Saed Ahmed owns two 10-year-old slave boys. He was asked by *Newsweek* magazine if there was racism or slavery in his country. He said, "There is no racism, there is no slavery."

Today, the United Nations International Children's Educational Fund or UNICEF (YOU-nee-sef), estimates that there may be 200,000 children sold into slavery each year worldwide. In April 2001, for example, 40 children were discovered in a ship that travels regularly between Benin and Nigeria. The movement of slave children goes on all the time, both on land and by sea. Even today, a kid can be bought in Cotonou (koh-tohn-NOO), the capital of Benin, for $30.

African Culture

What's an African like? That question is as hard to answer as "What's an American like?" Africans come in all shapes and sizes. Some are rich, and some are poor. Some are scientists; some are beekeepers. There are more than 1,000 ethnic groups or tribes in Africa. Even though we often see images of Africans similar to this photograph of three Dogon dancers during the yearly celebration of the beginning of creation, it is more common to see people like these young professionals.

The Dogon of Mali wear some of the most elaborate dance gear in Africa. These masks represent events at the beginning of creation and are used after five days of the spectacular *dama* funeral ritual.

Ceremonies

Africa has more spectacular and elaborate ceremonies than any other continent because there are so many different peoples living there. Over the generations, as bodies and facial features evolved differently among different groups, so did customs and habits. People everywhere like to feel that they belong to a particular group that is special and different from other groups. Just look at how Americans dress to support football teams or how Irish Americans wear green in a St. Patrick's Day parade. We all engage in rituals and adopt special costumes.

Maasai girls preparing for a wedding dance. Warrior admirers have given them their elaborate beaded necklaces.

African rituals and ceremonies, like other celebrations around the world, involve special behaviors that are repeated for particular purposes, often at special times. The special times may be seasonal, like the coming of the rains or the harvesting of crops—think of North American kids not so long ago dancing around the maypole in spring or families today eating a Thanksgiving feast in the fall. The events may also be important life milestones, like births and deaths. They may be a part of regular gatherings to worship, like Sunday mass in church or Friday prayers at the mosque. Or they may be for special problems; for example, to drive out an evil spirit from someone who is possessed. Europeans and Westerners have similar ceremonies. The Roman Catholic Church even today has an exorcism rite intended to chase the devil out of a possessed person or place.

Each ritual has its own costumes and equipment. Often special people lead the ritual in honor of a very special audience—like a god. There are probably as many types of ritual dances in Africa as there are ethnic groups. There are several reasons to hold a dance: asking for something (like rain), thanking for something (like a good harvest), worshiping God (or

Make a Ritual Elephant Mask

Make a ceremonial mask from papier-mâché. The term comes from French and means "mashed paper."

asks of all shapes and sizes are used to enhance the meaning of a ceremony or a dance. The Baoule people, who live in the Ivory Coast and in Cameroon, carve elephant masks from soft wood and paint them with pigments extracted from plants and soils. The elephant is a symbol of power and social stability. The mask is worn during general festivities to symbolize the power of the chief and to emphasize the order and stability of the group. In the past, dances were also done to encourage a successful elephant hunt, but today no one wants to encourage killing elephants, which are at risk of extinction.

You can make a Baoule-style elephant mask and organize your own ritual dance. You will build up a papier-mâché mask over a round frame (or armature) using an inflated balloon to provide the basic shape and using additional parts for the trunk, tusks, and ears made from sculpted pieces of chicken wire.

Adult supervision required

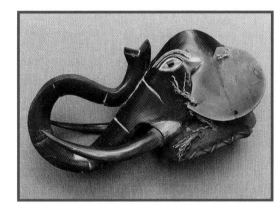

A Boule elephant mask from west Africa.

You'll need

Tin cutters

1 square yard of chicken wire

Pliers

2 mixing bowls

Wallpaper paste powder (fungicide-free; white baking flour can be used as a substitute)

PVA glue (a special water-soluble glue, available at a craft or hobby shop)

Old newspapers

Ruler

A long balloon inflated to 10–12 inches long (alternately, a squash or gourd about the same length)

Felt-tip marker

Masking tape

Paper towels

Pocketknife (or Exacto knife)

Scissors

Watercolor paints

Varnish or artists' fixative

String

1. Cut three long pieces (about 12 inches) of chicken wire and two more pieces about half that size. Twist and mold the larger pieces into the rough shapes of a trunk and two tusks. Twist the smaller pieces into ears. Set them all aside.

2. In a mixing bowl, mix a quart of wallpaper paste using the ratio 1 part wallpaper powder (or flour) to 10 parts water. In the second bowl, mix a smaller amount of liquid out of equal parts water and PVA glue.

3. Tear 20–30 one-inch-wide newspaper strips. Hold the paper down on a tabletop with the ruler and pull the paper edge back to the ruler to cut the strips quickly and cleanly. Put the strips into the wallpaper paste mixture and let soak for several minutes. Then dip the strips, one at a time, into the glue-water mixture.

4. Inflate the balloon to just a bit bigger than your head (it's a good idea to do this before your hands get sticky). Apply the soggy paper strips to the balloon, overlapping each strip by about one-fourth of its width. Crisscross the strips and cover the front three-quarters of the balloon to about three or four strips deep. Leave a rough hole in the back one-fourth of the mask where your face will eventually fit. Don't worry about rough edges; you will trim these later. Allow about 12 hours for the first layer to dry. Deflate and remove the balloon.

5. On the shell of the mask, mark the places where you will position the trunk, tusks, and ears, and cut out holes for the chicken wire armature pieces. Insert your chicken wire models, and bend the ends of the wire inside the shell to hold them fast. You may have to use masking tape on the inside to hold them in place.

6. Mix a fresh batch of wallpaper paste and the glue-water mixture, tear some more newspaper strips, and apply three to four more layers of papier-mâché over the chicken wire, spreading the ends of some strips onto the balloon shape.

7. Tear about 20 paper towel strips (more or less, as needed) and apply them over the whole mask as you did the newspaper (using wallpaper paste, then glue-water). Then use your fingers to mold bulges and ridges for the eyes, nostrils, "fingers" in the end of the trunk, wrinkles over the tusks, and any other decorative forms. Let the mask dry and set overnight.

8. Trim the face opening with strong scissors or a knife; bore two holes in the sides that you can thread a string through. Reinforce the holes on the inside with some masking tape.

9. Paint the mask, using any colors you like. When the paint is dry, varnish the whole mask and thread a string through the side holes in the mask.

Ruffle up your hair, put on the mask, and cover yourself with a large colorful cloth or blanket. Invite your friends over and ask them to chant a low, slow beat while you do an elephant dance to protect the African elephant from poachers.

Many Maasai prefer to wear their colorful and comfortable *shukas* today.

while another shoots a short arrow into the bulging blood vessel. They catch the blood in a gourd and shake it up with a little fermented milk and herbs. They pass the drink around so everyone can have some while it is still warm. Delicious!

This process does not seem to upset the cow. The small wound is plastered with mud, and the cow dashes off to rejoin the herd. Maasai love their cattle more than anything else and would never do anything to hurt them.

gods), and, of course, celebrating just for fun at events like parties or weddings.

African costumes are always colorful. The colors and designs are usually meaningful. Maasai are particularly fond of red. They cover themselves with red togas called *shukas*. The young warriors, called *il-morani* (EEL-moe-rahn-ee), decorate their faces and bodies with red ocher, a pigment derived from iron-rich red soils.

Why red? Because one of the Maasai's favorite meals is made from fresh blood tapped from the neck veins of their beloved cattle. One *moran* holds the cow's head and twists the neck to expose a vein,

Everyday wear in eastern Africa often includes colorful head scarves, and both women and men wear *kangas* (KAHNG-ga) as an outer garment. A *kanga* is a printed rectangle of cotton that usually has a Swahili proverb to match the pattern. A *kanga* covered with a pot design might include a pattern that reads "*Haba na haba hujaza kibaba*" ("little by little fills the measure"). Another might be decorated by a big circle that looks something like a breast and the saying "*Maziwa ya mama ni tamu*" ("mother's milk is sweet").

In the mid-1800s some style-conscious ladies of Zanzibar decided to make better use of the bandanas

Kanga Beachwear

There are hundreds of ways to wear a *kanga*. Here are a few simple variations that you can wear at the beach or while loafing around the house.

Africans are very inventive with their *kanga*s. They fashion them into skirts, dresses, shawls, pantaloons, baby carriers, shopping baskets, hammocks, beach blankets, and more. Try your hand at making various *kanga*s.

You'll need

Any colorful, light, cotton material, about 3
    feet by 4–5 feet

To make sure your *kanga* doesn't fall off, you need to learn basic folding and tying skills. These include:

pleating, for adjusting length and reducing bulges:

diagonal fold, for making headdresses and shawls:

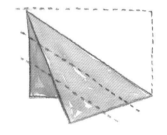

simple overhand tie for fastening two ends together and as steps in other knots, like the square knot:

square knot, for securely joining two corners or two kangas:

Girl's Traditional Head Scarf

Use the diagonal fold, follow the steps shown at right, finishing off with a square knot.

Girl's Neck-Knot Dress

This is the quickest way to get completely dressed. Wear the *kanga* horizontally, wrap around the front, and tie behind your neck.

Boy's Wraparound

This style is one of the simplest variations used by men and boys throughout Africa. Wrap the *kanga* around your waist and tuck in as you would a towel after a shower. Roll the tuck into the waist with a couple of turns and it will hold all day.

Males often prefer a bold striped pattern and slightly heavier cotton. In that case, the garment is called a *kikoi* (key-KOY). Today's African girls now wear them too, at the beach, for example.

(like cowboys and bikers wear) that were being brought by Europeans along with beads and metal utensils to trade for ivory and ebony. The ladies sewed six 18-inch bandanas together, two by three, to make a single piece of cloth.

When people saw the Swahili ladies wrapped in the latest fad, they were reminded of the noisy, social birds commonly found in the coastal bush, called guinea fowl. The birds are probably the ancestors of today's domestic chicken. The Swahili name for guinea fowl is *kanga*. Clever merchants started manufacturing cloth for the fashion craze with new designs and colors and Swahili proverbs. The name *kanga* stuck.

Coming of Age

Every African tribe has special celebrations and rituals to mark an individual's movement from childhood to adulthood. A coming-of-age ceremony is very important because it marks the time when a person can begin to become a productive member of the community. The rituals are usually complicated and time consuming, and many of them involve circumcision.

This procedure is not the kind of medically supervised circumcision that is still performed on more than one million American male infants each year. No, millions of African kids each year endure a much more painful procedure.

The Maasai of Kenya and Tanzania, for example, circumcise both boys and girls. The ritual begins at dawn. A boy, 14 to 18 years old, has cold water splashed over him and is taunted with insults from his friends. The purpose of this part of the ceremony is to help him build up courage for the ordeal to come, for he must endure the cut without crying out or flinching to prove his bravery and to be accepted into the comradeship of his age group. If he cries out, he will be shamed for the rest of his life.

Although the ordeal is painful, it helps build unity among boys of the same age group because they are circumcised at more or less the same time. After circumcision, they all wear black and fashion elaborate headdresses decorated with the feathers of small birds that they shot with bows and arrows. The young men roam around together in a gang for a few weeks. The whole experience bonds them into a group and they will support each other for the rest of their lives, first as warriors and later as tribal elders.

What happens to a girl is far more extreme and far more painful. Without anesthetic, she has parts of her sex organs removed by an old woman who acts as the circumciser. Unlike her brothers, she is allowed to cry out without shame, which of course she does, begging the female relatives who are holding her down for help. They don't help her. In fact, they participate willingly, believing it's all for the best.

The girl is given a milk cow and other gifts by her father to honor her new status as a woman. The girl is probably not very interested in presents at that particular moment. She is wrapped in a dark blue shawl, given a special beaded headdress to wear, and

Demons and Shadows

Demons are everywhere in African mythology and appear frequently in fables, like animal characters. Unlike Western demons, which are usually evil henchmen of the devil, African demons are powerful spirits who punish wrongdoers and ward off the evil eye. However, if a bad person makes a deal with a demon, the demon can be used to harm someone else. The Makonde tribe of Tanzania carves fantastic demons out of African ebony. The type of demon pictured here is called *shetani* (shey-TA-nee), meaning "devil" in Swahili. They are designed to throw spooky shadows from the firelight on the inside of the walls of a hut to chase away evil spirits. Can you see the face in the shadow?

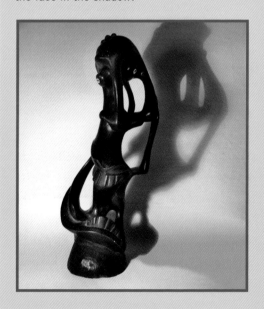

goes off to recuperate for some days. She is now ready for marriage.

Female genital mutilation (FGM), as it is called, has been performed on nearly 150 million African women living today. Each year two million girls endure the ritual, which has been performed for generations and is deeply rooted in cultural tradition, although the practice is beginning to be shunned by many modern Maasai.

Many modern social workers and doctors in Africa are working to have the practice of FGM replaced by less cruel and dangerous rituals to celebrate coming of age. Some tribes, like the Krobo in Ghana, practice a far less painful and much more joyful coming-of-age ritual. Krobo women are considered to be the most beautiful women in west Africa. The ceremony to mark their entry into womanhood is called the *Dipo*. It is a celebration of femininity and fertility that has been practiced for over 800 years. At the start of the *Dipo*, each girl in the group enters a special ritual hut, sheds her childhood dress, and is measured for new clothes by her ritual mother, usually an aunt. She is given a belt made of a single strand of quartz beads to hold a long red cloth that passes between her legs and hangs nearly to the ground in the front and back. The red cloth is a symbol of menstrual blood.

The girls' heads are then shaved, leaving only a little tuft of hair on the back. Their heads are rubbed with a mixture of charcoal and shea butter. The shea (SHAY) tree is a west African tree that bears particu-

Krobo girls chatting at a wedding.

larly oily nuts. The group then goes into seclusion for three weeks, during which time they are taught traditional ways of preparing food, grooming themselves, dancing, and other useful skills they will need as adults.

At the end of the period, they are given white cloth head scarves and loincloths to replace the red ones and are paraded to a special grove of trees near the village. Each girl has a leaf put in her mouth to keep her from chatting and to help her think seriously about her changing status.

Before the final part of the ritual, two priestesses test the girls' virginity by splashing their stomachs with a sort of holy water and making them sit on a white *tekpete* (tek-PAY-tay) stone three times. Three more priestesses judge if the girls are "pure." If they pass the test, they leave the grove, with each girl carried on the back of a parent or guardian, who dashes back to the village under a volley of gunfire sent up by the men. The girls are escorted, because in ancient times there was a real danger that men from other tribes hiding in the forest would kidnap them on the way. Back at the village, the girls are decorated with strings of yellow beads and presented to the community as women.

Language and Writing

Western colonialists used to say that there was no African written culture until 150 years ago when white missionaries started making written records of African languages. The oral tradition—the practice of passing tribal facts and history down from generation to generation through the spoken word—and storytelling have always been important in Africa. These practices work well in cultures where old people live with the family until they die and where there are few modern devices that we take for granted, like pens, notebooks, tape recorders, and computers. But, in fact, written language has existed in sub-Saharan Africa longer than in Europe.

In the Ethiopian highlands by A.D. 400, the citizens of the Axum Empire were already using a written language called Ge'ez (GAY-ez, with a pause between syllables), which is the only alphabet entirely developed in Africa. Even English and most other European languages borrowed from the ancient Roman alphabet.

Recently, in the ancient city of Timbuktu in northern Mali, Western scholars discovered manuscripts written by a black historian named Mahmud al-Kati. He lived in the mid-1300s, more than 100 years before Columbus reached the Americas. The Timbuktu scholars used Arabic to write about history, law, and religion. But they also adapted the Arabic alphabet to make written forms of local tongues, like Fula.

Some slaves brought writing skills with them to America. Umar ibn Sayyid, who was held in bondage in North Carolina, wrote his life story in Arabic. His skill was troublesome for the slave owners, who wanted to spread the notion that Africans were illiterate savages.

How many languages do North American kids speak? Most speak English and many also speak the language of their communities, like French in parts of Canada, Spanish or a Native American tongue in many parts of the United States, or the languages of many other ethnic communities such as Greek, Chinese, Armenian, and so on. A few may know a third language, because they have studied French or German or Hebrew in school.

There are over 1,300 tribal languages spoken in Africa, more than on any other continent. These languages are the first tongues of most Africans, yet most African kids know at least three languages. Take, for example, Kenyan kids of African origin (as opposed to kids of Indian or European origin, of which there are many in Kenya). All will certainly speak one of the tribal languages that they have spoken at home since birth. In school they learn English, the official language of government and business that is a leftover from British colonial rule. In the schoolyard they speak Swahili, which is used as a common language throughout eastern Africa. On the streets, many will probably pick up Sheng, a kind of hip-hop mixture of Swahili, English, Hindi, and tribal tongues.

There are other official languages of African governments that reflect colonial history, such as Arabic, French, Spanish, and Portuguese. Ethiopian and Eritrean governments use only the ancient Amharic language. The Somalian goverment uses both Arabic and the country's main language, Somali. Tanzania declared Swahili its official language. South Africa has eleven official languages: English and Afrikaans plus nine tribal languages. Afrikaans is a Dutch language that was the tongue of the *vortrekkers* (FOUR-treckers, meaning "those who trekked before"), a group of people from Holland who settled in South Africa in the 17th century. Each month in the South African parliament, government business is conducted in a different language, and proceedings are translated into all the other languages. The parliament sits for half the year in Cape Town and half the year in Pretoria. They have recently added sign language to the proceedings. The nine tribal languages are also taught in South African schools.

A lingua franca (LING-wa FRANK-a) is a common language that is used by many people who have different first languages. (It's an Italian phrase that means "Frankish language," a language that traders used to understand each other at the crossroads of the Middle East hundreds of years ago, that was a mixture of Italian, French, Greek, Arabic, and Spanish.) Today, English is the most common lingua franca in the world.

Tic-Tac-Toe: The First Game?

The simple game that kids play with friends when they should be listening in class has its origin at the beginning of human speech in Africa, maybe 100,000 years ago. Some experts believe that the first human word was something like *tik*, meaning "finger" (*tik* still means finger in some Eskimo tongues—remember, the ancestors of Eskimos migrated out of Africa tens of thousands of years ago). *Kidole* (key-DOUGH-lay) is Swahili for finger or toe, and it's no accident that there's a similarity of sound with "toe." *Dik* means "one" in the sub-Saharan language of Fur, and the smallest antelope in the East African grasslands is called the dik-dik, which is almost always seen in pairs: one-one. You can imagine being an African kid, 50,000 years ago, playing tic-tac-toe in the dirt with a friend, just like they do today on pieces of paper in the schoolroom. Maybe an ancient rule stated that you make the *X*s with your finger and the *O*s with your big toe.

Click Languages

The San Bushman, Hottentot (HOT-ten-tot), Zulu, Swazi, and Xhosa (GHOW-za) peoples of southern Africa all speak languages that are classified among the "click" families of languages: Khoisan or Nguni. They are called click languages because many of the consonants in their alphabets are spoken by clicking the tongue off the roof of the mouth. The Sans' native name for themselves is !Kung, where the "!" represents a click. A Khoisan speaker can incorporate as many as 15 different clicks in a word by snapping the tongue off different parts of the inside of the mouth: the back, middle, and front of the palate; the side teeth, like clicking a horse to giddyap; the front top teeth, like saying "tsk, tsk"; the pursed lips; and the throat, which is nearly impossible for nonnative speakers. Try them, and try to say "!Kung" with a click instead of a *k* sound. Can't do it? Tsk, tsk.

Africa is a continent of lingua francas, probably because it has so many tribal and official languages. Arabic is used throughout north and northeast Africa, French in most of west Africa, Swahili in eastern Africa, along with English, which is also spoken and taught in most southern countries. In other areas, one particular tribal language may become a lingua franca between neighbors, like Lingala in the Congo or Hausa and Bambara in west Africa.

A Fulani girl living in northern Nigeria might speak Fula as her tribal language. She learns English in school and also has a good working knowledge of two lingua francas—Arabic and Hausa—from playing with other kids in the neighborhood.

Even though different peoples often fight and compete with each other, sharing a lingua franca is a sure sign that they are trying to get on together, and in the future, probably will.

Africa Today and Tomorrow

So far, adults have called the shots, but now it's time to build the world with children. Your voices will be heard, I promise.

—*Kofi Annan, UN Secretary General*

New Governments

There are 53 independent countries in Africa, from Algeria in the north to Zambia in the south. Many have had stormy histories over the past 40 years. For many, the fight against colonialism was an armed conflict. For others, the fighting continued after independence as rival groups killed each other to gain control of the government. Some African leaders are now proposing that all African countries consolidate into the United States of Africa, but the differences between countries are probably too great for that to happen soon.

Some countries have produced great leaders, the equivalent of George Washington and Thomas Jefferson. Others have been unfortunate enough to have horrible dictators.

Idi Amin (EE-dee ah-MEAN) was a Ugandan soldier who became chief of the army and air force in 1966. He disagreed with president Milton Obote

"President for life" Idi Amin wanted to show how important he was by being carried around by four British businessmen.

How to Say "Hello"

Africans are very polite. When Swahili speakers greet another one, they exchange common greetings like "hello" and "how are you," but then they go on to ask about each other's families and the weather at home. They talk about all kinds of things before going their separate ways or discussing the reason that they're meeting.

A conversation between Swahili speakers may go like this:

"*Hujambo?*" ("You have any affairs going on?")

"*Sijambo!*" ("No, I've got nothing much going on.")

"*Habari?*" ("What news? Everything OK?")

"*Mzuri. Habari yako?*" ("Good; everything's fine. What's your news?")

"*Mzuri, tu. Na habari za wazee?*" ("Just fine. And how are your folks?")

"*Wazuri wote. Labda zako?*" ("They're all fine. How're yours?")

"*Njema. Habari ya nyumbani?*" ("All excellent. How are things at home?")

"*Mzuri kabisa, lakini tunangoja mvua.*" ("Terrific, except that we are waiting for the rains.")

"*Hata sisi, laikini itakuja karibu.*" ("So are we, but the rains will come soon.")

"*Bila shaka unasema kweli. Habari nyigine?*" ("Without doubt you are correct. What other news?")

"*Mzuri tu, lakini . . .*" (All's well, except . . . ")

Note that the first speaker confirmed once again that everything is good, *mzuri* (mm-ZOO-ree) (*tu* is added for emphasis), but then he adds "except," *laikini* (lie-KEY-nee) . . . He will probably tell his friend that although he is pleased to report that things are fine in general, in fact, his house just burned down, his family's crops were all eaten by locusts, and a large rock fell on his grandfather. It is considered very rude to jump right into bad news.

By the way, there are many words in most African languages that begin with an *m* or an *n* followed directly by a consonant: *mzuri* (good), *ngini* (more, other). These are rather difficult for Westerners to pronounce. The trick is to sort of hum the *m* or *n* sound: mm-ZOO-ree, nn-GEE-nee, with a hard *g*, as in "goat." Try to say in Swahili, "The good person wants more bananas": "*Mtu mzuri anataka ndizi ngini*" (Literally, "Person good he/she does want bananas more." The word order sounds a bit odd in English, but in Spanish or French you also find adjectives following nouns.) Say: MM-too mm-ZOO-ree a-na-TA-ka nn-DEE-zee nn-GEE-nee. Easy, eh?

Become a Painter in the Naïve School of Art

Who needs a canvas? African artists paint on just about anything: a length of timber, a piece of cardboard, or the side of a box.

Some African artists paint simple and very colorful pictures. Painters around the world who use this style belong to a school of painting called Naive (nie-EVE), meaning simple, straightforward, sometimes with a bit of humor. Naive painters, like the Americans Grandma Moses and Horace Pippin, are often untrained in formal drawing. They don't care too much about making the painting look exactly like its subject, like a photograph or a representational drawing. They often use wonderfully bright colors and ignore perspective, which is how an artist makes some parts of the painting look near and other parts far away.

In Ghana, Naive artists have joined forces with coffin makers to produce individualized coffins. The family of a deceased fisherman, for example, might order a coffin shaped and colorfully painted like a fish.

African Naive painters usually use animals as their subjects because there are so many animals to choose from and because animals have characteristic colors and shapes.

You'll need

Old newspapers

A picture of an African animal

2-by-2-foot piece of hardboard (or any piece of wood with a flat surface, like a length of 12-inch board, the side of a packing crate, or, in a pinch, a piece of thick cardboard).

10-ounce cans of poster paints: red, blue, green, yellow, black, and white

Paintbrushes: 3-, 1-, and ½-inch

A couple of pieces of chalk

A few jam jar lids for trying out color mixes

Bucket of water

2 small nails (or eye hooks)

Hammer or screwdriver

3-foot length of thin wire

A few rags

1 can of turpentine for cleaning brushes and mopping up spilled paint

Clear varnish (a spray varnish is easiest, but liquid varnish will also do)

1. Spread newspaper on the floor or on a table in a well-ventilated place and place your piece of wood on the newspaper.

2. Choose one color for the background. Black or red are often popular with Tanzanian Naive artists, but you may also want to use green if you've chosen a herbivore like a zebra as your subject. Paint the board evenly using the three-inch brush.

3. When the background color is dry, use the piece of chalk to make a sketch of your subject. Don't try to make it look too realistic. In fact, the more stylized the better. Ask yourself, what are one or two really striking characteristics of your subject animal? For example, elephants are big and round with amazing trunks, big ears, and tusks; zebras have striking black-and-white stripes; hornbills, storks, and ibis are all big birds with large beaks; rhinos have big horns on their noses; crocodiles have rows of impressive teeth; and so on. Emphasize those striking characteristics and don't worry much about the other details of the animal.

4. Using the chalk, sketch a few minor subject decorations around the main subject. Funny-looking, colorful birds are popular. You may want a couple of trees with simple leaves, round fruit, and branches for the birds to sit on. Naive artists often repeat the same minor subjects around the edges of their paintings.

5. Using the smaller brushes, fill in the colors of the major subject. Be inventive. Don't feel constrained to paint a rhino gray or an impala brown. Make the rhino purplish or the impalas bright orange. It's your call.

Tip: you probably know that you can use mixtures of primary colors (red, blue, and yellow) to make all kinds of other wonderful colors. Red + blue = purple. Blue + yellow = green. Yellow + red = orange. Add some white to a reddish purple and you get a flamingo pink. Experiment by mixing a little of each color in a jam jar lid. Don't mix too many colors or you'll get the color of mud.

6. Remember to clean your brushes well in a bucket of water after applying each color; otherwise, the next color will start to look muddy. Naive artists like pure colors.

7. You may need to let some of the big patches of color dry before adding details in different colors. Naive painters tend to keep the lines between colors sharp and well defined. In fact, you may want to emphasize a particular part of your subject by drawing a thin black or white line around while holding the 1/2-inch brush sideways.

8. Once you're happy with your painting of the main subject, turn to the minor subjects and the decorations around the sides. Use other colors, perhaps more white, and repeat patterns. The smaller brushes will be useful.

9. When you're happy with the colors and the designs, let the whole thing dry for several hours.

10. Spray a layer of clear varnish over the whole painting. Let dry, then apply a second coat. (If you are using varnish in a normal can, use a clean three-inch brush.)

11. When the painting is completely dry, turn it over on a piece of newspaper to protect the paint, and tap or screw in the two small nails or eye hooks onto either edge of the back side. Stretch the thin wire tightly between the two attachment points and wrap it around each one. A good rule of thumb is to attach the wire about one-third down from the top of the painting. Thus, if you had used a two-foot by two-foot piece of hardboard, you would put the nails (or eye hooks) eight inches from the top edge.

12. Clean up your paintbrushes and work space with the rags, bucket of water, and turpentine.

13. Hang your painting for all to see and admire.

President Bokassa crowns himself emperor of the Central African Republic.

and led the army to overthrow the government. He declared himself president and chief of the armed forces in 1971, field marshal in 1975, and president for life in 1976. He persecuted and killed people who weren't members of his Kakwa tribe. He ordered that 300,000 Ugandans be killed by being thrown into the Nile for crocodiles to eat and by being hit on their heads to save bullets. He hated intellectual people, so he drove most of the good teachers out of Makerere (mah-KAY-reh-reh) University, which used to be one of the best in Africa. He expelled all citizens of Indian origin from Uganda in 1972. Many of these citizens were important businesspeople, and without them, the Ugandan economy collapsed. He publicly insulted Great Britain and the United States.

Amin was overthrown in 1979 by Ugandan and Tanzanian troops and lived in exile in Saudi Arabia until he died in 2003.

Jean-Bédel Bokassa (ZHAN-bay-del bow-KAH-sah) was president of the Central African Republic from 1966 to 1979. Like Idi Amin, he was an army commander who took over the government by force. He abolished the constitution, fired a lot of qualified ministers, and gave himself more and more power until he declared himself emperor, just like his hero Napoleon Bonaparte. He spent $200 million of the country's money on his coronation party and then built himself a huge palace out in the bush. It nearly bankrupted the country. He committed horrible atrocities during his reign, including participating in

How to Be a Bad President

Take over power from a previous leader by force.

Give all the good jobs in the government to your friends and relatives.

Don't let anyone criticize you in the newspapers; shoot anyone who criticizes you really badly.

Encourage tribalism by giving special rights to your tribe, and make sure that people from other tribes don't have a chance to get ahead.

Take a large part of the money that industrialized countries (like the United States) give you to fix the roads or build hospitals and send it to your personal bank account in Switzerland.

Export most important agricultural crops, like maize, sugar, and flowers, for your own profit.

Import a lot of cheap stuff, like clothes, electrical appliances, or honey, from other countries to make money for yourself even though it leaves your own citizens poor.

Make all the important decisions by yourself.

Declare yourself president for life.

Blame the fact that your citizens are starving on (a) the drought, (b) the old colonial government, (c) the neighboring country, or (d) all of the above.

How to Be a Good President

Take over power from a previous leader in a free and fair election.

Give jobs in the government to the most qualified people.

Encourage a free press and open public debate.

Provide equal opportunities for all your citizens.

Invite foreign investors to support development activities in all parts of your country.

Make certain that your citizens have enough food for themselves before the surplus is exported to other countries.

Encourage the development of local industries and farms so your citizens can make a good living.

Delegate responsibility to your most qualified assistants.

Don't stay in office until you are too old to be a good leader.

Plan ahead and learn from history by (a) building up an agricultural surplus to feed your citizens during a drought, (b) taking the best practices from the old colonial government and adapting them to your people's needs, (c) negotiating with neighboring countries for them to buy your surplus products and for you to buy theirs.

cannibalism and in the massacre of 100 schoolchildren. He was overthrown with the help of French troops, and a new president took over. After a while, that one, too, was overthrown in a military coup.

Léopold Senghor (seng-GORE) was elected the first president of Senegal in 1960. He had been educated in France and was the first African to reach the highest level of teacher in that country. He fought with the French army during World War II and was held captive in a Nazi concentration camp, where he wrote poetry. He has published many books of poems and was the first black scholar elected to the French Academy. He formulated the idea of "negritude," which became an important cultural movement of French-speaking African and Caribbean writers who supported the value and dignity of black culture and history. Senghor was a kind man who modernized the agricultural system in his country and was beloved by his people and respected by other governments. He retired voluntarily from the presidency in 1980.

Julius Nyerere, first president of Tanzania, was fondly known by his people as Mwalimu (mwa-LEE-moo), meaning "teacher" in Swahili. He studied at Makerere University in Uganda (before Idi Amin's policies ruined it) and was the first Tanzanian to get a master's degree in history and economics from a British university in Edinburgh. He organized adult literacy programs and established free education for all. Tanzania still has one of the highest literacy rates in Africa. He tried to improve agri-

President Léopold Senghor of Senegal.

Mwalimu Julius Nyerere, the first president of Tanzania, who served from 1964 to 1985.

cultural production and emphasized that Tanzania must become economically self-sufficient rather than depend on help from foreigners. He was a botanist. He invented a system of cooperation within villages called *ujamaa* (oo-ja-MAH), meaning "familyhood" in Kiswahili. It was a socialist system in which all property, land, and agricultural production was owned in common by the people in the village. Sadly, it failed, perhaps because many people preferred not to share. Nyerere was a true idealist, and like Senghor, a gentleman and a scholar. He wrote several books and translated plays by Shakespeare into Swahili.

Today, most African countries are democracies. Kenya, for example, held an election at the end of 2002, and a new president from the opposition party was elected peacefully. Governments are clearly changing for the better.

Africa Is Poor

Sadly, despite the continent's long and rich history, mineral wealth and beautiful landscapes, and fantastic plants and animals, African countries are among the poorest on earth. The United Nations measures every country's ability to provide its citizens with a decent standard of living through the Human Development Index (HDI). An index is used to calculate a number that expresses the level of something. For example, a doctor uses the body temperature index as a first check for illness. The HDI is a composite index because it combines several other indexes of health, education, and wealth. (Does the United States come out on top? No. The United States is in eighth place, after Norway, Sweden, Australia, Canada, the Netherlands, Belgium, and Iceland.)

Healthiness is measured indirectly, for example, by an index measuring life expectancy at birth, a number that is an estimate of how many years on average a person born in a certain place can expect to live. The index includes health-related measurements such as infant mortality and the availability of health services. The country with the highest life expectancy in the world is Japan, with 82 years. The lowest is a horrifying 34 years in Sierra Leone (see-ER-ah lee-OWN) in west Africa. The life expectancy of people born in the United States, by the way, is 77 years.

Education is measured through adult literacy (how many grown-ups can read and write) and enrolment in schools. At the top end are North American and European countries, where more than 99 percent of adults can read and write. At the very bottom is Burkina Faso (burr-KEY-no FAH-so) in west Africa, with only 16 percent. Imagine what it would be like if only about one in seven of your friends could read and write?

Wealth is measured by an index called Gross Domestic Product or GDP ("gross" because it's uncorrected and rough, "domestic" because it refers to what citizens buy for the home and family, and "product" because it calculates many measurements, like the product of a multiplication problem). GDP is the total value of goods produced and services provided by a country. The GDP divided by the number of people in the country provides a rough estimate of how many dollars each citizen can spend in a year. The highest in the world is Luxembourg, with $61,000 per person (there are fewer than 400,000 people there, and they are all pretty rich). The United States is fourth, with $36,000. The lowest in the world is—again, in Africa—Sierra Leone at $520.

Of the 53 countries in Africa, all are close to the bottom of the 2004 HDI list. Look at the HDI world map. Most of the countries with a low HDI are in Africa, and not one has a high index. This means that of all the governments in the world,

those in Africa are least able to provide a decent way of life for their people.

Why does Africa score so low when it comes to health, education, and welfare? There are many complicated reasons for the state of affairs in Africa, including poverty brought on by a lack of job opportunities, a lack of personal assets such as land and capital, limited access to credit, environmental degradation, wars, and corruption.

So is Africa a hopeless case? No. The continent has produced many success stories. Of the 43

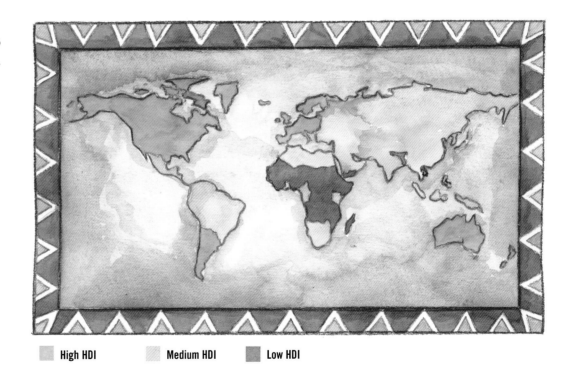

High HDI   Medium HDI   Low HDI

Human Development Index world map, 2000.

War Zones

In 22 of the 53 countries in Africa, a war was raging in 2005. The fighting usually occurs between rival groups who want to control the government or force some of the people to behave like the rest, for example, by practicing the same religion. Does this mean that Africans are more violent than other people? Certainly not. In the rest of the world, at least 40 other countries are fighting for the same reasons.

In fact, there is little or no archaeological evidence that suggests Africans fought among themselves in the past any more frequently or more violently than any other groups of humans. Violent conflicts became common in Africa with the arrival in the 1400s of Europeans who brought guns and greed for the riches of Africa: gold, ivory, exotic plants and animals, and slaves.

Of course, in the early part of the first millennium (which spans year zero to the year 1000), as cattle herding became more and more important, people acquired surpluses of animals, lived well, and became healthier, and more children survived childhood. The population started growing rapidly, and where there are more people, there are more opportunities to fight over land, cattle, religion, or power.

African countries for which there are reliable data, 28 have improved their HDI since 1995, compared to 15 in which the HDI has decreased or has not changed. In some countries, at least, things are looking up.

Three African Kids

Meet three very different African children who all live in Kenya. They are all 12 years old. The first one is named Mwangi (mm-WAHNG-ee, a common name in the Giguyu tribe in Kenya), after his grandfather. He is one of the 20,000 street kids who live in Nairobi. There may be as many as 100,000 in the whole country. He never met his father. His mother died last year of HIV/AIDS. He is lucky that he did not get AIDS at birth like so many other street kids. Mwangi has no family and no home. He sleeps on a collapsed cardboard box under a road viaduct in downtown Nairobi.

In the morning Mwangi begs for pennies along Nairobi's main street. There are so many other street kids that the competition is fierce. Mwangi is only the size of a 10-year-old, so he usually loses fights for money or food, unless he's fighting a smaller kid. He can often find something to eat in the garbage pails behind hotels and restaurants, so he uses the pennies he has begged or stolen to buy some glue.

Why glue? At night, Mwangi and a few other street kids gather around a fire sniffing glue out of discarded plastic medicine bottles. Glue fumes can cause a high that help a sniffer like Mwangi forget

Afri-Facts

In 2000, there were 794 million Africans (compared to 240 million Americans).

Thirteen out of every 100 people in the world are African.

The African population is growing almost twice as fast as the rest of the world.

One out of every seven Africans is a Nigerian.

Though the continent is so large, it is relatively underpopulated: one person per acre is the average as opposed to nearly two people per acre over the rest of the world.

Africa is the only continent in which the people are expected to get poorer over the next century.

Sixty percent of African adults can read and write (the world average is 75 percent).

The number of undernourished Africans doubled between the 1960s and 1995, to 200 million.

Africa has lost 190,000 square miles of tropical forest since 1980, an area about the size of all of Central America.

Twenty-five African countries will not have enough water by 2025.

Every African country has mobile phones, Internet access, and satellite TV.

about the gnawing hunger in his belly. The glue also destroys his brain cells.

The city of Nairobi recently started a program to help kids like Mwangi. With luck, he may start to go to school soon. His life may also improve if he becomes involved with one of the local charities like the Udungu Boys Center (oo-DOONG-oo, meaning "brotherhood" or "fellowship" in Swahili). If he can stay off glue and learn a craft like metal- or woodworking, he may then get a *jua kali* job (see page 113) making items like pots or chairs. Otherwise, he may be dead of brain damage or disease before he is 18 or become a criminal trying to avoid getting caught or even killed by the police. Mwangi doesn't have many choices yet.

My father uses his weekends for sleeping and smoking. I sympathize with his situation. He doesn't always go to work. He is always in bed as he doesn't know what to do after he wakes up.

—Susan Muthoni, Nairobi street kid

A Kenyan kid named Kananu (ka-NA-noo) is far better off than Mwangi. She lives with her family on their *shamba* (SHAHM-bah, meaning "farm") 100 miles north of Nairobi on the slopes of Mount Kenya. The farm is very small, with only a quarter acre of land. Kananu's father was one of four brothers who divided up their father's small holding when the old man died. Kananu's mother comes from the other side of the mountain near Embu. She's a wa-

Meru, a tribe not too different from the Giguyus. Kananu is the middle child: she has three older sisters and had three younger brothers. Sadly, the youngest died last year of tuberculosis.

The family grows vegetables, mainly corn, beans, and potatoes, for home consumption. For cash, they plant a small patch of pyrethrum (pie-REE-thrum), a little white daisylike flower that can be processed into an organic pesticide. In a good year, with enough rainfall, they can sell their surplus crops in Karatina, the nearest market town. The family also has one milk cow and a small herd of sheep and goats.

Kananu's first task after she gets up at five o'clock in the morning is to muck out the sheep and goat pen. She then drinks some sweet, milky tea and eats a bowl of *uji* (OO-gee), which is a thin gruel made of corn meal, sugar, and, if the family cow is producing, milk. Otherwise, water. *Uji* is the main breakfast of nearly every kid in East Africa.

Kananu's main job, when she's not working on the *shamba*, is to help her elder brother lead the grazing sheep and goats along the edge of the main road, then up a river valley, nearly to the Mount Kenya forest edge. It's a pretty interesting trip, since she can see lots of different kinds of cars and trucks on the road and lots of animals and birds along the river. Once she and her brother even saw an elephant about a mile from the forest. They had run with their livestock all the way home.

If next year is a good year and her father can sell the pyrethrum, Kananu will start going to the local

Hot Sun Business

There are very few salaried jobs available for the large number of young people in Africa. If they don't want to be beggars or thieves, the thousands of people without work have to become *jua kali* (JOO-ah KAH-lee, meaning "hot sun" in Kiwahili) workers. They work outside in the open making whatever will sell from whatever materials are available. Scrap metal is cut and beaten into pots, wheelbarrows, charcoal cooking stoves, spoons, and dozens of other household utensils. Discarded wood from packing crates makes chairs, stools, tables, and cupboards that are sold at reasonable prices to people who have little money.

Africa's Last King

I am tired of being poor; I want to be a queen. I hope the king sees me.

—Nomsa Gama, Swazi 17-year-old

Nomsa was one of 50,000 young women who danced in front of King Mswati III (mm-SWA-tee) and his warrior guards during the annual weeklong reed dance ceremony in September 2003. Each year, girls ages 10 to 18 dance for the 30-something-year-old king, hoping that he will choose them to be one of his brides. It's said that the king reviews the videotapes of the dance taken by the local TV station in order to make his yearly selection. He currently has a dozen wives. He is called the Lion, and the Queen Mother Ntombi (nn-TOME-bee) is known as the She-Elephant. The Swazis believe that it is the king's duty to have as many wives and raise as many kids as possible. Mswati's father, King Sobhuza II (soab-HOO-za), had 65 wives and over 100 children.

According to Swazi mythology, the first human beings sprang out of a large swamp reed split lengthwise. So the girls collect reeds on the way to the ceremonial grounds in the Mdzimba Mountains, split them with long knives, and carry them in bunches during the dance to symbolize the strength, unity,

and prosperity of the Swazi nation. Afterward, they offer them to the queen mother to reinforce the fence around her compound on the royal palace grounds.

A lot of people criticize this old-fashioned practice. The mother of one dancer claimed that her daughter was later abducted by palace guards from her schoolyard and forced to join the royal household against her will. Some women's rights groups have protested and demanded that the reed dance be stopped. What do you think?

The Swazi king and his royal guards.

Country kids on the way to school. Most kids in Africa wear school uniforms. For the poorest ones, wearing a uniform means not having to be ashamed of shabby everyday clothes.

school. Her younger brother will take over herding, except on the weekend. Kananu will still do farm chores in the early morning and when she comes back from school.

If she does well at school and gets help from family friends in a *harambee* (har-ahm-BAY, meaning "pull together" in Swahili) fundraiser (see page 121), Kananu may eventually go to secondary school. University is a much more remote possibility; very few kids off the *shamba* ever get there. And even if they do finish, there are so few jobs that their futures are not very rosy.

A third kid, Njoroge (NN-joe-row-gay, another common name, a bit like George), has a different story altogether. Njoroge lives in a three-bedroom house covered with bougainvilleas in a Nairobi

African Beadwork

In this project you'll make a beadwork "love letter" necklace, similar to the one the king of Swaziland is wearing on page 114. To keep things simple, your necklace will have only one panel.

Africans use beads to decorate lots of items, including articles of clothing, hats, belts, shoes, furniture, utensils, and themselves, wearing ornaments from earrings to anklets. Originally, beads were made from natural materials collected locally or traded with other tribes. These materials included mollusk shells, seeds, ivory, ostrich eggshells, wood, clay, and bone. Later, glass and metal became important, but the colors were still drab. When the 18th- and 19th-century explorers brought brightly colored glass "seed" beads from Europe, the local craftspeople got very excited. At last, really flashy colors!

In the Yoruba tribe of Nigeria, men are in charge of beadwork. In other groups, like the Ndebele of South Africa or the Maasai of East Africa, the women are the experts.

You'll need

1,200 beads (half should be yellow, 200 each in red, black, and white)

Strong black thread

Small needle

Clear nail polish

3 larger, ¼-inch white wooden beads (any of the other above colors, and plastic will do)

1. To tie on the first bead, string the black thread through the red bead twice (diagram 1)

Don't make a knot because double threading does the trick. Leave a six-inch tail of thread for finishing off. Then, alternately thread yellow and red beads to make a total of 30 beads on the first row.

2. For row two, thread one red bead (row two will use half the number of beads as row one, all red) onto the necklace. Thread the next bead through the second-to-last bead of the previous row, threading the needle in the opposite direction as row one (diagram 2)

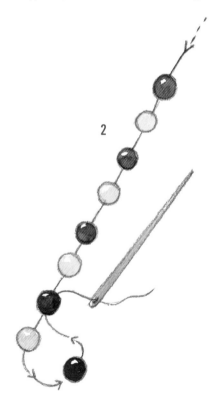

115

Thread on another red bead and thread through the fourth-to-last bead of row one. Repeat threading in this way (back up through the 6th, 8th, 10th, etc., bead from the end) until all 15 beads of row two are in place (this is called the peyote stitch in modern beadworking jargon).

3. Row three will be done in the same way, except you will thread in the opposite direction. For rows four and five, repeat as above using yellow beads (diagram 3). Obviously, you will want to tighten your stitching to eliminate spaces between beads (spaces are left in the diagram for illustration only).

4. For row six and the rest of the rows, continue threading beads following the pattern in diagram 4.

5. To make the string of beads fit around your neck, you will need to have at least 18 inches of string left when you finish the final row.

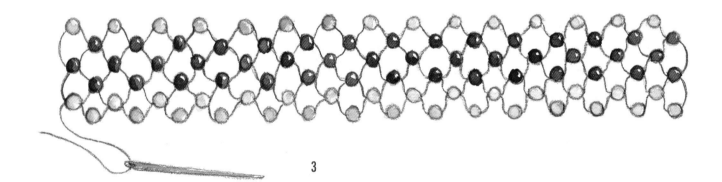

3

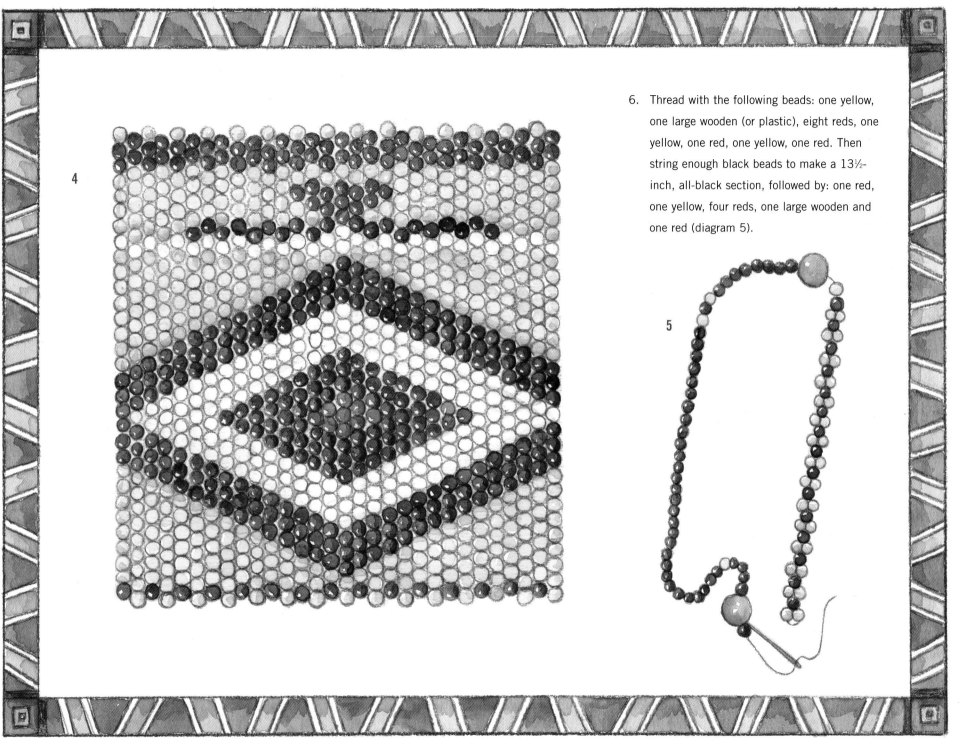

4

6. Thread with the following beads: one yellow, one large wooden (or plastic), eight reds, one yellow, one red, one yellow, one red. Then string enough black beads to make a 13½-inch, all-black section, followed by: one red, one yellow, four reds, one large wooden and one red (diagram 5).

5

7. Finish off by threading back through the wooden bead (leave the last red bead snug up against the wooden bead) and several red beads. Tie a couple of knots over the main thread, cover with a drop of nail polish, and thread the remaining tail back through more beads. Trim.

8. To make the fastening loop, tie a new thread onto the free corner on the top of the love letter by threading between two corner beads, tying a knot, and leaving a three-inch tail. Thread on the following beads: 1 red, 1 wooden, 13 reds. Thread back through the first of the 13 beads, the wooden bead, and the first red bead (diagram 6).

Check that the loop fits snugly over the wooden bead in the end of the neck strap. Knot the end of the thread tightly with the tail. Cover the knot with a drop of nail polish and, when the polish is dry, finish off by threading back along a nearby row.

9. Wear it yourself or give the love letter necklace as a gift.

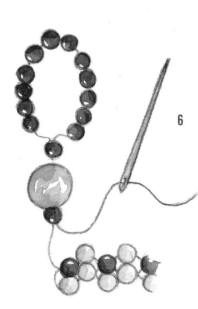

6

suburb. His father is a lawyer who was educated in London and is now a program director for a United Nations agency that has an office in Nairobi. Now that the two eldest kids have left the family home, Njoroge's mother has gone back to work for the University of Nairobi teaching community health. Njoroge's eldest sister, who is also a lawyer, works in the United States and is married to a businessman.

The middle sister is still at a university in northern England studying medicine. Njoroge's elder brother Charles, who is 18 and thinks he's the coolest person in the world, is in his last year at a private high school, where his father went. Charles is OK, though, since he lets Njoroge use his computer to surf the Web when he's not using it.

In a nutshell, Njoroge is lucky enough to live like any other privileged kid in the world. He can eat nearly anything he wants for breakfast, and he's got a mountain bike, an MP3 player, and Nintendo games. He goes to a private school, and he will almost certainly go to college.

The trouble with this picture is that for every kid in Njoroge's situation, there are 10 in Mwangi's.

Extended Families

A kid's life in rural Africa, that is, a kid who is not a member of a well-off family in town, is very different from a kid's life in the West. Extended families are the most common social unit. Extended relatives are important in most families throughout the world—grandparents, aunts, uncles, cousins—

Members of an extended family in Kenya.

except in Africa, extended family members all live in pretty much the same place. If not in the same village, then probably not more than a day's walk away from each other. A six-hour walk to visit a relative is nothing for an African kid.

Family titles like "auntie" and "uncle" are also used for close family friends. Often aunts and uncles, whether real or by adoption, participate in

Mitumba

Selling secondhand clothes is one of the biggest businesses in Africa. It's called *mitumba* (me-TUM-bah), which means "bales," like the bales of cloth that traders used to carry around on their camels. Many Western people donate perfectly good clothes before they wear them out. But such secondhand clothing does not necessarily go to local charities. Tons of used clothes are sent from the United States and Europe by middlemen collectors to dealers in Africa, who distribute them to street vendors, who in turn sell them to the public. It's not unusual to see a girl who earns only $10 a month as a housemaid wearing Calvin Klein jeans on her day off or a barefoot street kid in a grubby Harvard University sweatshirt.

Although the *mitumba* industry makes Western clothes available to poor people, it has two big downsides. One is that it destroys local textile manufacturers because the secondhand imported clothing is much cheaper than locally made clothes. The other is that the profits from *mitumba* in some central African countries are suspected of supporting rebel groups who are at war with the government.

raising kids, keeping them in their homes for long periods and teaching them useful things like how to skin a goat or how to dig in a sand river to find water. African families put a strong emphasis on loving and supporting all children in the community.

Children take on a big share of family chores and often have responsibilities that would seem daunting to Western kids. Imagine getting up every day at five o'clock in the morning and lighting the cooking fire. A girl could also be expected to spend the morning looking after her infant brother or sister. It's not unusual to see a girl just seven or eight years old with a baby strapped on her back.

African extended families follow unwritten rules that demand cooperation and sharing within the family. If a person is in trouble or in need of something, a member of the extended family will help out, and vice versa. If an African walks to a distant cousin's village for a visit, the cousin will certainly invite the visitor in to share a meal and spend the night. But the family obligation can also be a hardship. If a family member gets a good job in the city, he or she will feel obligated to send most of the salary back to the family in the bush and will have dozens of close and distant relatives asking for loans. This can make it hard to get ahead.

Corruption

Ask anyone on the streets of Lagos or Nairobi, what is the biggest problem in your country? Nine out of 10 will answer, "corruption!"

There are many kinds of corruption, and probably everyone has committed a corrupt act at one time or another. Stealing an eraser, not admitting to having done something bad, or not completing a task you were paid to complete as well as possible are all forms of corruption. Corruption on a small scale at home or school may give a person a few enemies or hurt a few feelings; corruption on a large scale can ruin a whole country and make the lives of millions of people miserable.

Corrupt government officials behave dishonestly in many ways. They might steal some of the money that is supposed to be used for public works like road building. Or they might complete a task in a sloppy way and accept payment as though it had been done well, for example, by using cheap steel to build a bridge but charging for the good-quality steel. Or they might secure a powerful job in the government and then give themselves a nice piece of land, like a park that really belongs to all the citizens.

Companies that bribe government officials in order to get jobs are also corrupt. One year alone, 80 percent of Uganda firms paid bribes just to do business.

Corruption is common in Africa. An organization called Transparency International studies corruption around the world. Only 14 of Africa's 53 countries scored more than 5 points on their corruption scale, which ranges from 1 (most corrupt) to 10 (squeaky clean). But remember, corruption is not just an African problem; it's a human problem.

Harambee!

It is common in Africa for people to lend each other helping hands. In Kenya, the business of providing a helping hand has become a national institution called *harambee*. Say, for example, a family has a sick member who needs an operation or a bright student who needs funds to start secondary school. The family will slaughter a couple of goats, cook up vegetables, brew maize meal beer, and invite the neighbors over for a social gathering and a sing-along. Toward the end of the party, the father will make a little speech about the sick family member or the bright young student and then pass the hat for contributions. Everyone contributes something, no matter how little, because the neighbors all know that one day they might have to do the asking.

The first president of Kenya, Jomo Kenyatta (JOE-mow ken-YAH-tah), turned the tradition into a political rally call to encourage his people to work together to build the new country. At the end of every one of his speeches, he would raise his fly whisk and get the crowd to shout in unison three times: *Harambee! Harambee! Harambee!*

Some practices that seem corrupt to Westerners may just be part of African culture. For example, in many traditional African tribes as well as in medieval Europe, it was customary for ordinary citizens to pay a tribute to the leaders. This tribute could be as simple as removing one's cap to show respect or as costly as giving a leader one-tenth of the annual grain harvest. So it's not surprising that the early leaders of new African nations felt no qualms about pocketing some of the national wealth, and the citizens took for granted that leaders would get rich. That's just part of being a leader, or so it used to be.

But taking some tribute sometimes leads to taking more and more, particularly when the law is not enforced vigorously. Today, the citizens of many African democracies are fed up with corruption, and demand greater transparency from their leaders. This means that the leaders must conduct their business openly and not sneak the nation's wealth off to secret Swiss bank accounts.

Many countries now have anticorruption departments that are trying to clean up the governments by uncovering wrongdoing and forcing the law to prosecute the wrongdoers. The international organization Transparency International uncovers corruption and makes a lot of noise about corrupt activities to try to embarrass governments into making their officials more honest. And, perhaps even more importantly, the citizens are starting to demand honesty and fairness from their elected politicians.

Women's Rights

African women have traditionally been treated as second-class citizens. Most African societies are patriarchal. This means the family group is ruled by a father or an old man who serves as the family patriarch. Not only are women and girls lowest on the pecking order, they are also made to do all the cooking, cleaning, and hoeing of the fields. In rural parts of Africa it is common to see a man strolling along the roadside, swinging his walking stick, with his wife walking 10 paces behind him carrying a 50-pound load of firewood or bananas on her back.

Violence against women is also common, and wife beating persists among country and city folks. Despite enduring this treatment, women often become the heads of rural families when men go to the cities to look for work or are killed in armed conflicts.

But times are changing: women are demanding their rights. Women's groups are now active in nearly every African country. In 2002, 10 women won senior Kenyan government positions. In 2004, Wangari Maathai became Africa's first woman to win a Nobel Peace Prize, for her environmental work with rural communities. And in 2005, Ellen Johnson-Sirleaf was elected president of Liberia, making her the first female president of an African country. Gender equality, like racial equality, is an important step to social reform and good government.

Citizens Take Action

In 2002 the citizens of Kenya elected a new president, Mwai Kibaki (mm-WHY key-BAH-key), and voted out the old government. Everyone is now hoping governmental corruption will stop. Ordinary citizens have started pitching in to help. Here's one example that was originally reported in the *Daily Nation* newspaper.

In Kenya, most people go to and from work in a taxi called a *matatu* (mah-TAH-too; *tatu* means "three" in Swahili, maybe because the taxis can always fit three more customers). *Matatu* drivers drive like crazy, pushing other cars out of the way, stopping in the middle of the road, and speeding from stop to stop to grab customers before the next *matatu* comes along. Some drivers will cram 25 commuters into a 12-seater taxi. *Matatu*s are owned by rich people who want to get richer, so they pay the drivers by the number of customers the drivers transport and spend as little as possible on keeping the *matatu*s in good shape.

For years, traffic cops have flagged down *matatu*s and made a big show of the car's bald tires or cracked windshield or the driver's expired license. The driver then talked on the side with the cop and slipped him *kitu kidogo* (KEY-too key-DOUGH-go, meaning "something small," like the equivalent of a dollar or two in shillings, the local currency).

But during a recent incident, when a cop took his usual 100-shilling ($1.25) bribe, all the passengers jumped out of the *matatu*, emptied the astonished cop's pockets of all his takings for the day, and marched him off to the nearest primary school. They then made him hand over all his bribes to the head teacher to buy milk for the kids' lunch.

The story spread around the country, and now traffic police are being very careful and really inspecting and fining faulty *matatu*s.

Cities

Many Westerners think that most Africans live in grass huts. In reality, one out of every three Africans is a city dweller. Africans have been moving to urban areas for as long as Europeans have been moving to cities. Timbuktu and Djenne (jen-AY) in Mali have been occupied for 1,600 years. Like people worldwide, Africans have the tendency to move to cities to look for jobs and escape the tough life of farmers or herders. The downsides of this migration, as in cities everywhere, are crowding, disease, pollution, and increased crime.

Dumping rubbish anywhere, anyhow, has become a habit in African cities today. We are running out of places to dump our garbage. How can we force our generation to re-use, recycle, and repair their possessions to achieve the most important goal, which is to reduce the amount of garbage they generate?

—Jennifer Chanda, a Zambian teenager

Lagos, Nigeria.

There are 15 cities in Africa with more than two million inhabitants, cities about the size of Tampa or Vancouver, British Columbia. There are two so-called megacities of over 10 million people, Lagos and Cairo. Although these cities have tall office buildings, they also have terrible slums. For every one white-collar office worker, there are 10 slum dwellers.

The Mathare houses are made of cheap materials like sticks, stones, polythene, papers, rags, and metal tins. To stick them together they use mud. The biggest house is eight-by-eight feet, where a family of seven to ten lives in one room that is partitioned by bed sheets. Apart from that the slum looks good.
—Beldine Achieng, a 14-year-old kid who lives in the Mathare Valley slum in Nairobi

HIV/AIDS

By the year 2010 there will be 40 million orphans in Africa. Why? Because today there are more than 30 million parents who are likely to die soon because of HIV/AIDS, a disease that destroys the body's natural defenses against disease. If the orphans are lucky, they will be able to move in with their grandparents or an aunt. If they are unlucky (as most of them are bound to be), they will be forced to live on the streets as beggars or will be captured and forced to fight for an army or rebel group. Many will die of AIDS themselves. In 2006, out of every ten 15-year-olds in Botswana, eight will likely die of AIDS. In some parts of southern Africa, one person in every three has AIDS.

Scientists believe that the HIV virus started in west African monkeys. Viruses can change very quickly to adapt to new places to live, and it is possible that they jumped from monkey to human, for example, when someone killed and ate infected bush meat (see page 28).

Is there any hope? Governments need to do more. Western governments and drug companies need to make cheaper medicines available for Africans. African governments need to provide better food and nursing care to keep infected mothers and fathers alive longer. Without much more aid money, Africa cannot afford drugs, food, or nursing supplies. Only about one in every 8,000 infected Africans can afford anti-HIV drugs. The United States announced in early 2003 that it was going to reduce the costs of the drugs in Africa. This sounded like good news at the time. But even though $15 billion was set aside for the Emergency Plan for AIDS Relief, anti-HIV drugs are still too expensive. In Kenya, for example, the drugs cost $10 a day, yet the average Kenyan earns only about $360 a year. He or she can hardly afford to spend everything on medicine. As a result, HIV/AIDS is still a death sentence in Kenya.

Child Soldiers

In 1985, a religious fanatic named Alice Auma claimed that a Christian spirit named Lakwena pos-

What African Kids Are Saying About Why Young People Get AIDS

Njooko, the Gambia:

"Our leaders have not done enough to arrest the infection. They prefer to fight over diamonds here and there especially in the African continent. Do not sit and watch the whole young population of the world being wiped out. Whom will you govern then?"

Dingile Chibambo, Zambia:

"Since my country . . . is a third world country, I think the Government must give free education and shelter to the children who have lost their parents because of HIV/AIDS. . . . These children also need entertainment and recreation and this can only be provided with the help of the government, business community and individuals."

Bismark Firang, Ghana:

"I think lack of good moral education is a major cause. In Africa in general and in Ghana in particular, there used to be good traditional systems of educat-ing the youth on the consequences of premarital sex which to some extent worked. But with so many inter-cultural influences as a result of globalization, all these have died out. We in Africa therefore need to sit up and see how best we can incorporate these good cultural values into our educational systems."

Osesenaqa Lekgoko, Botswana:

"Being a young woman in the southern part of Africa, one of the problems that other girls face is the problem of tradition. The rest of the world might be living in the modern age but back here many are facing problems of lack of education. This leads to igno-rance concerning AIDS and how it can affect them. The longstanding tradition of parents not talking to their children also poses a problem as the kids are not informed or worse yet misinformed about AIDS and the dangers it holds. If these strong traditional links could somehow be broken or even modified then the war would be half won."

sessed her and instructed her to form the Holy Spirit Mobile Forces to fight for equal rights of the Acholi tribe. Like a possessed Joan of Arc, Alice of Lakwena decided that the best way to rule Uganda was by following the Bible's Ten Commandments while also capturing children and murdering people. President Museveni's Ugandan Resistance Army defeated her in 1998, but another fanatic, Joseph Kony, claimed he took over Lakwena's spirit, and he formed the Lord's Resistance Army (LRA) to brutally carry out the mission.

Late one night in 2001 a band from the LRA stormed into Amina's home and carried her off in the dark. The LRA was recruiting. During Amina's 35 days of military training, she was forced to kill a boy who tried to escape. She witnessed another boy being hacked to death for not raising the alarm when a friend ran away. She was beaten when she dropped a water container and ran for cover under gunfire. She was raped. She was sent off to fight against adult soldiers of the Ugandan government army. More than 300,000 children under 18—some as young as 10—are fighting in armed conflicts in more than 30 countries worldwide. Thirteen of the 22 African countries in which there are wars going on use kids as soldiers.

There are so many modern, lightweight weapons available in the world that kids can be efficient and obedient killers in combat. Child soldiers are often made to fill special roles, such as spies, messengers, sentries, porters, servants, and even sexual slaves. Many children fight on the front line alongside adult soldiers. Others are used to clear land mines. Children are often forced to commit acts of violence against their own communities or even families. This makes them feel like outcasts and traps them even deeper in the army way of life. They are given drugs and alcohol to numb their minds.

I would like you to give a message. Please do your best to tell the world what is happening to us, the children. So that other children don't have to pass through this violence.

—Amina, 15-year-old former rebel soldier in Uganda

Why are so many weapons available in the world? Because weapons trading is such lucrative business, and arms manufacturers make a great deal of money. The five permanent members of United Nations Security Council (China, France, Russia, the United Kingdom, and the United States) are responsible for four out of every five small arms exports to the rest of the world. Two out of every three American guns go to developing countries. The United States is one of the world's largest producers of land mines and so far has refused to sign an international treaty to ban their use.

Thirteen African countries—Algeria, Angola, Burundi, Chad, Congo, the Democratic Republic of the Congo (formerly Zaire), Eritrea, Ethiopia, Rwanda, Sierra Leone, Somalia, Sudan, and

War games? No, real wars, and kids are forced to be soldiers.

Uganda—are known to have government armies or rebel groups that forcibly recruit child soldiers.

President Joseph Kabila (kah-BEEL-ah) of the Democratic Republic of the Congo ordered the country's armed forces to demobilize child soldiers and stop recruiting minors. He said the government would stop recruiting children under 18 and would no longer send them to the front lines to fight the rebels. He admitted that child soldiers had been used in Congo's successive wars, and he declared that it was the government's duty to help them back into society.

Hunger

How many kids reading this book have ever been hungry, really hungry? Probably not many. But try to imagine hunger pangs that rarely go away. Try to

Only Elephants Should Wear Ivory

There are now about 300,000 elephants in Africa. That may sound like a lot, but just 20 years ago there were over one million. Poachers have killed huge numbers of elephants for their tusks. If they are allowed to continue poaching, elephants will disappear before this generation's grandchildren have a chance to see them in the wild.

There is now a policy battle raging about the international trade in ivory. One side, particularly groups from southern Africa, say that they need to sell the ivory that is found in the bush on elephants who died naturally. They need the money to maintain parks and support the human communities around the parks.

Those may sound like good reasons, but the people who argue against the ivory trade believe that if any trade at all is allowed, illegal poaching will continue. And then, everyone will have to spend far more money than what is earned in ivory sales to fight poachers. They argue that it's better not have any trade at all.

What is done with all the ivory that's collected? Well, at least one country had a pretty drastic solution: Kenya burned a 10-ton pile of ivory. If poachers knew that's what will happen to ivory, it wouldn't be worthwhile to kill elephants.

Can you think of a better solution?

imagine an almost constant pain in your belly and head. Try to imagine feeling weak and sleepy and cold all the time. Sound strange? Not to the nearly four out of every ten kids in Africa who are constantly hungry and undernourished.

If a person is hungry and weak, he or she is more likely to get sick. Most deaths among African children under five result from one or more of five common ailments: dehydration from diarrhea, measles, chest infections, malaria, or starvation. Treatment for these ailments doesn't cost much but simply isn't available to thousands of poor, rural Africans.

And here's the really amazing thing. There's actually enough food in the world to go around; it's just that some people have lots and others don't have enough. In fact, the World Health Organization calculates that there are more people in the world who are overweight than people who are starving. In developed countries, 20 percent of the population is overweight. In Africa and other developing countries, not more than one in 20 people are overweight.

No one is smart enough to know how to end world hunger, but Joel Cohen, the director of the Rockefeller Population Institute, suggests that the answer must have something to do with a bigger pie, fewer forks, and better manners. What do you think he meant by that?

Conservation or Development? Or Both?

Although much of Africa is a wonderland of exotic plants and exciting animals, all is not well with the environment. Rapid population growth, increased pollution, and overuse of resources like trees and water all contribute to an environmental crisis. Africans are, of course, aware of these problems. Every African country today has a department or ministry of the environment. Many Africans live close to the soil, so they know more about how the environment is doing than many Western people. But they have a dilemma.

When poverty overrides everything else, people forget about the environment.

—Ayub Osman, Kenyan 16-year-old

Honest African leaders are desperately trying to make sure their people have enough to eat, clean water, basic education, and the opportunity to get a job and raise a family in peace and security. They rightly say to people from Europe and North America who hassle them about protecting nature, "You dare to ask me to protect this forest because it is a world treasure? I have hungry citizens who need to make a living there. If you want us to preserve the forest for the trees, elephants, butterflies, biodiversity, or whatever, then you should pay for it."

Environmental destruction continues at such an incredible rate not because people act foolishly, but because large numbers of people are poor. Until corrupt politicians stop stealing from their own people, until developing countries can sell their crops and manufactured goods at competitive prices, until unscrupulous people stop exporting the best each country has to offer, until developed countries stop trying to make huge profits by selling—instead of sharing—drugs and technology, until all that happens . . . then most Africans will continue to be poor, and surviving will be more important than protecting the environment.

The Nelson Mandela Story

On July 25, 1918, a son was born to the third wife of the hereditary chief of the Tembu tribe in the Cape Province of South Africa. That boy, Nelson Mandela, grew up to become one of the greatest leaders of our time.

Like many bright kids of the day, Mandela went to a Methodist mission school. He was an eager student and excelled in sports like boxing and long-distance running. Maybe these sports helped him develop bravery and tenacity to endure what life had in store for him. He went on to study at a university to get a law degree and joined a political party called the African National Congress (ANC) in 1944. He immediately got involved in the resistance movement against the ruling party's racial policies of apartheid (see page 89). The apartheid government recognized him as a potential threat and arrested him several times.

At first, Mandela urged passive resistance to apartheid. However, after a brutal incident in a Johannesburg suburb named Sharpeville in which 69 unarmed blacks were killed and 189 injured, he

Nelson Mandela, the first black president of the Republic of South Africa.

127

reluctantly began to support the use of more violent means of protest.

Mandela and the ANC party worked in secret and hid from the ruling party. There was one big difference between South Africa and the other African countries in the 1960s. Other countries were struggling to free themselves from colonial rulers who had only been in charge for 70 to 80 years. These colonial governments finally moved back to London or Paris. In contrast, the white South Africans had been running the government and farming the land for 300 years; there was no way they would agree to pack up and go. In South Africa, change would have to come from within.

Every revolutionary movement needs leaders and a small band of followers brave enough to break repressive laws. Just think of the Boston Tea Party. Or Mahatma Ghandi's nonviolent, noncooperative protests against British rule in India. Or the four brave young black Americans who, one day in 1960, plunked themselves down at a whites-only lunch counter in Alabama.

Mandela's underground activities threatened the apartheid government. When he came back from a 1962 trip to Algeria—which was illegal because non-whites couldn't travel outside the country without permission—he was arrested and thrown in jail. At the end of the trial, Mandela said, "I have fought against white domination, and I have fought against black domination. I have cherished the ideal of a democratic and free society in which all persons live together in harmony and with equal opportunities. It is an ideal which I hope to live for and to achieve. But if needs be, it is an ideal for which I am prepared to die."

Additional charges of sabotage were added, and the initial five-year sentence became life. Mandela was imprisoned under maximum security on Robben Island, a prison a couple of miles out to sea from Cape Town.

Over the years, Mandela became a symbol of the struggle against oppression in South Africa. Although he wasn't tortured or beaten, he was occasionally put into solitary confinement. He rejected several government offers to allow him to leave prison on the condition that he renounce violence in the freedom movement.

The outside world became disgusted with apartheid. South Africa became isolated. Nobody wanted to do business with South Africa, and no one wanted to travel there. Inside South Africa, a new generation of people of all colors came to realize that there is no future in a system where one group represses another. As Mandela said some years later:

> I am also here today as a representative of the millions of people across the globe, the anti-apartheid movement, the governments and organizations that joined with us, not to fight against South Africa as a country or any of its peoples, but to oppose an inhuman system and sue for a speedy end to the apartheid crime against humanity.
>
> These countless human beings, both inside and outside our country, had the nobility of spirit to stand in the path of tyranny and injustice,

without seeking selfish gain. They recognized that an injury to one is an injury to all and therefore acted together in defense of justice and a common human decency.

Early in 1990 Nelson Mandela was released as a free man after 27 years in prison. Twenty-seven years! Think about it—that's almost half an adult lifetime. Most people would have felt terribly angry with the people who had been jailers and looked for ways to get back at them. But not Nelson Mandela. The next year, at the first legal gathering of the ANC in 30 years, Mandela related his vision of a new South Africa where all races and cultures lived on an equal footing. The years of prison had not hardened him. He forgave the wrongdoings of the past and his oppressors. He led South Africans of all colors into a new era of democracy.

In 1992, Mandela won the first free and fair election in South Africa and became its first black president. The year after, the world honored him with the Nobel Peace Prize, which he shared with F. W. de Klerk, the country's last white president, who was also brave enough to stand up against apartheid.

Watch This Space

Here's a question: how long should it take a newly established country to "get its act together"—to stop corruption and to develop an independent legal system to ensure that laws are fair, and to provide citizens with health, education, and the chance to be happy?

For example, 95 years after its independence, America engaged in a bloody civil war. It took another 100 years for the civil rights movement to eliminate segregation. Those battles in the United States of America spanned a total of 200 years.

And that was relatively quick and not half as bloody as the emergence of European countries. Over the last 500 years in Europe, one war followed after another and fighting continued relatively recently in Northern Ireland and the former Yugoslavia.

Most African countries have only been independent since the 1960s, for just over 40 years. Isn't it a bit unfair to criticize relatively young African countries for not learning in just one generation what Westerners have taken 10 or more generations to figure out (and what many argue they have not perfected even yet)?

One might hear someone say, How long will it take these people to get their act together? It's going to take a very, very long time, because it's really been a whole series of interruptions and disturbances, one step forward and two or three back. It has not been easy. One always wishes it had been easier. We've compounded things by our own mistakes, but it doesn't really help to pretend that we've had an easy task.

—Chinua Achebe, Nigerian novelist

An Activity for the Year 2060

Do you think you can remember to do something several decades from now? Try writing a letter to yourself and storing it somewhere safe for years to come.

To the kids reading this book today, let's give Africa 100 years—half of what the United States had—to "get its act together." After the year 2060, when most African countries will have been independent for about a century, take a few moments to judge for yourself how Africa is doing.

Examine the human development indexes of African countries.

Ask yourself: Has infant mortality dropped to below 10 in 1,000? Are the armed conflicts in certain counties over? Have HIV/AIDS and malaria been eradicated? Has Cameroon, Senegal, Kenya, and South Africa each won the football World Cup? Do "peace parks" exist to give wild animals a chance to move across national boundaries? Is there enough food and water to go around? Are the central African forests intact? Have elephants, gorillas, and chimps (and hopefully whales, too) been saved from extinction? Are African kids better off?

Finally, give the continent a grade. Hopefully it's an *A* for Africa.

There is a place where the grass meets the sky, and that is the end.

—*Maasai saying*

Resources

Selected Bibliography

Croze, Harvey, and John Reader. *Pyramids of Life*. London: Harvill Press, 2000.

Diamond, Jared. *Guns, Germs and Steel: The Fates of Human Societies*. New York: W. W. Norton, 1997.

DiSilvestro, Roger P. *The African Elephant: Twilight in Eden*. New York: Wiley, 1991.

Lamousé-Smith, W. Bediako, and Joseph School. *Africa Interactive Maps*. CD-ROM, version 1.0. Baltimore: University of Maryland, 1998.

Mandela, Nelson. *Long Walk to Freedom*. London: Abacus, 1995.

Marnham, Patrick. *Fantastic Invasion*. New York: Penguin, 1987.

Mazrui, Ali A. *The Africans: A Triple Heritage*. London: BBC Publications, 1986.

Middleton, John. *Africa: An Encyclopedia for Students*. New York: Charles Scribner's Sons, 2001.

Oliver, Roland. *The African Experience: From Olduvai Gorge to the 21st Century*. London: Phoenix Press, 1999.

Owusu, Heike. *Symbols of Africa*. New York: Stirling Publishing, 2000.

Pakenham, Thomas. *The Scramble for Africa 1876–1912*. London: Abacus, 1991.

Reader, John. *Africa: A Biography of the Continent*. New York: Alfred A. Knopf, 1998.

Roberts, Allen F. *Animals in African Art: From the Familiar to the Marvelous*. New York: Museum for Africa Art, 1995.

Sampson, Anthony. *A History of South Africa*. London: HarperCollins, 2000.

Willertt, Frank. *African Art, An Introduction*. London: Thames and Hudson, 1971.

Woolcombe, D., ed. *Pachamama*. London: Evans Brothers Ltd for UNEP, 1999.

Web Sites to Explore

AllAfrica
http://allafrica.com/
AllAfrica is a current news site that compiles and indexes content from more than 300 sources (these outside sites are responsible for their own reporting and opinions).

Breaking the Silence: Learning About the Transatlantic Slave Trade
www.antislavery.org/breakingthesilence/index.shtml
This site aims to help teachers and educators to break the silence that continues to surround the story of African enslavement that began over 500 years ago. It provides teachers with a variety of resources and ideas about how to teach the subject holistically, accurately, and truthfully.

The Coalition to Stop the Use of Child Soldiers
www.child-soldiers.org/
The Coalition to Stop the Use of Child Soldiers works to prevent the recruitment and use of children as soldiers, to secure their demobilization, and to ensure their rehabilitation and reintegration into society.

Human Rights Watch
www.hrw.org
Human Rights Watch is dedicated to protecting the human rights of people around the world. It helps victims and activists to prevent discrimination, to uphold political freedom, to protect people from inhumane conduct in wartime, and to bring offenders to justice. See in particular the section on street kids (www.hrw.org/children/street.htm) or the exposé on government-sanctioned violence in Darfur, Sudan (www.hrw.org/doc/?t=africa_pub&c=sudan).

MBIRA—The Non-Profit Organization Devoted to Shona Mbira Music
www.mbira.org/index.html
Mbira is a nonprofit organization whose purpose is to educate the public about the traditional Shona music of Zimbabwe, which includes mbira music, and to develop a library of recordings to preserve it.

The Institute for International Mediation and Conflict Resolution (IIMCR)
www.iimcr.org
The IIMCR is a Washington, D.C.-based nonprofit institution whose mission is to promote the use of peaceful conflict-resolution techniques among a generation of future leaders.

National Museum of African Art
www.nmafa.si.edu/
The National Museum of African Art is a branch of the Smithsonian Institution in Washington, D.C. It is dedicated to advancing an appreciation and understanding of Africa's rich visual arts and diverse cultures, since, as it says in the mission statement, Africa, the cradle of humanity, is part of everyone's heritage.

Play Mankala
www.imagiware.com/mancala/
www.lookoutnow.com/game/mancala.htm
www.manqala.org/
There are many Web sites devoted to the ancient board game mankala. You can visit the three sites listed above, or you can use an Internet seach engine to find others. On most of them you can play an interactive, online game with a computer.

The Population Reference Bureau, Sub-Saharan Africa
www.prb.org/template.cfm?template=InterestDisplay.cfm&InterestCategoryID=246
For 75 years, the Population Reference Bureau has been providing timely and objective information on worldwide population trends and their implications, including child exploitation and female genital mutilation.

PBS Africa for Kids
http://pbskids.org/africa/index.html
This site contains many high-quality, interactive resources for sharing African schoolchildren's experiences: you can listen to folk tales, make thumb pianos and masks, and more. Teachers who want to provide an interactive classroom experience can use the four lesson plans for grades 3–12 in the Teacher Tools section. This site makes it easy to explore such topics as African ecology, ethnicity, society, culture, and economics.

Human Development Report 2003: Millennium Development Goals: A Compact Among Nations to End Human Poverty
http://hdr.undp.org/reports/global/2003/
The Human Development Report compares different countries' progress in the areas of health, education, and welfare.

UNAIDS—Joint United Nations Programme on HIV/AIDS

www.unaids.org/EN/default.asp
UNAIDS aims to lead, strengthen, and support an expanded response to HIV and AIDS that includes preventing transmission of HIV, providing care and support to those already living with the virus, reducing the vulnerability of individuals and communities to HIV, and alleviating the impact of the epidemic.

UNICEF—Voices of Youth

www.unicef.org/voy/voy.html
For 25 years, UNICEF (originally called the United Nations International Children's Emergency Fund) has worked for the survival, development, and protection of children. The UNICEF Voices of Youth Web site explores, reports, and asks kids to comment on youth-oriented issues such as education, sexual exploitation of children, HIV/AIDS, poverty, and much more.

UN Special Session on Children, May 2002

www.un.org/ga/children/
In May 2002, more than 7,000 people participated in the most important international conference on children in more than a decade, the Special Session of the UN General Assembly on Children. People from all over the world committed themselves to improve the situation of children and young people. The Web site presents information about what happened at the Special Session as well as the follow-up actions that have been taken to implement the official declaration and plan of action for "A World Fit for Children"; these actions include the Convention on the Rights of the Child (CRC) and the Global Movement for Children. Be sure to check out the special "Under-18 Zone."

Books to Read

Abrahams, Roger. *African Folktales*. New York: Pantheon, 1983.

Achebe, Chinu. *Things Fall Apart*. London: Heineman, 1958.

Beatty, Theresa M. *Food and Recipes of Africa*. New York: Powerkids Press, 1999.

Bigham, Elizabeth. *Fun with African Beads*. London: British Museum Press, 1999.

Cook, David, and David Rubadiri, eds. *Poems from East Africa*. London: Heineman, 1971.

Courlander, Harold. *A Treasury of African Folklore: The Oral Literature, Traditions, Myths, Legends, Epics, Tales, Recollections, Wisdom, Sayings, and Humor of Africa*. New York: Marlowe & Company, 1995.

Dinesen, Isak [Karen Blixen]. *Out of Africa*. New York: Random House, 1938. Reprint, New York: Penguin, 1985.

Eldon, Kathy. *The Journey Is the Destination: The Journals of Dan Eldon*. San Francisco: Chronicle Books, 1997.

Frobenius, Leo, and Douglas C. Fox. *African Genesis: Folk Tales and Myths of Africa*. New York: Dover, 1999.

Greaves, Nick. *When Elephant Was King and Other Elephant Tales from Africa*. Cape Town: Struik Publishers, 2000.

Greaves, Nick. *When Hippo Was Hairy and Other Tales from Africa*. Cape Town, Struik Publishers, 1989.

Gurnah, Abdulrazak. *Paradise*. New York: Penguin, 1995.

Hanby, Jeannette, and David Bygot. *Kangas: 101 Uses*. Nairobi: Haria Stamp Shop, 1992.

Kipling, Rudyard. *Just So Stories*. London: Macmillan & Co. Ltd., 1902.

Markham, Beryl. *West with the Night*. London: Virago Press, 1986.

Ngugi wa Thiong'o. *Weep Not Child*. Nairobi: East African Educational Publishers Ltd., 1964.

Paton, Alan. *Cry, The Beloved Country*. New York: Penguin, 1958.

Smith, Alexander McCall. *The No. 1 Ladies Detective Agency*. New York: Abacus, 2002.

Thesiger, Wilfred. *Arabian Sands*. New York: Dutton, 1959.

Watson, Lyall. *Warriors, Warthogs and Wisdom: Growing Up in Africa*. London: Kingfisher, 1997.

Index